CW01346187

Karma Yoga
The Art of Working

This book is dedicated to my Holy Father and Divine Master, H.H. Bhagavatpada Acharya Mohan Swarupa Shukla, a great Bhakta and Scholar of Vedism, whose inspiration helped me all my life and transformed me into the depth of the Vedic Culture
Om Shantih, Shantih, Shantih Om

Karma Yoga
The Art of Working

A Commentary on the
Third Chapter of Shrimad Bhagavad Gita

Shri Prabhuji

UBSPD
UBS Publishers' Distributors Pvt. Ltd.
New Delhi • Bangalore • Chennai • Kolkata • Patna • Kanpur

UBS Publishers' Distributors Pvt. Ltd.

5 Ansari Road, New Delhi-110 002
Phones: 3273601, 3266646 • Cable: ALLBOOKS
Fax: 3276593, 3274261 • E-mail: ubspd@ubspd.com
Website: www.gobookshopping.com

10 First Main Road, Gandhi Nagar, Bangalore-560 009
Phones: 2253903, 2263901, 2263902 • Cable: ALLBOOKS
Fax: 2263904 • E-mail: ubspdbng@bgl.vsnl.net.in

60 Nelson Manickam Road, Aminjikarai, Chennai-600 029
Phones: 3746222, 3746351, 3746352 • Cable: UBSIPUBS
Fax: 3746287 • E-mail: ubspdche@eth.net

8/1-B Chowringhee Lane, Kolkata-700 016
Phones: 2441821, 2442910, 2449473 • Cable: UBSIPUB
Fax: 2450027 • E-mail: ubspdcal@cal.vsnl.net.in

5 A Rajendra Nagar, Patna-800 016
Phones: 672856, 673973, 686170 • Cable: UBSPUB • Fax: 686169
E-mail: ubspdpat1@sancharnet.in

80 Noronha Road, Cantonment, Kanpur-208 004
Phones: 369124, 362665, 357488 • Fax: 315122
E-mail: ubsknp@sancharnet.in

Distributors for Western India:
M/s Preface Books
Unit No. 223 (2nd floor), Cama Industrial Estate,
Sun Mill Compound, Lower Parel (W), Mumbai-400 013
Phone: 022-4988054 • Telefax: 022-4988048 •
E-mail: Preface@vsnl.com

First Published 2002

Cover Design: Miss Melissa, Brisbane, Australia

Printed at: Rajkamal Electric Press, Delhi

ACKNOWLEDGEMENT

The author wishes to express his appreciation to all those who have helped to prepare this book for publication. Millions of Adorations and Gratitude to Gurudev Paramahamsa Omkarananda Saraswati, a born Mystic and Sage, a Philosopher of transcendental Wisdom, a Saint of universal Love, a Philanthropist of manifold Services to Mankind, who gave His blessings to start the whole work and encouraged everybody who helped in one or the other way to get this book done in the way it is just in front of you. Special thanks go to Swami Chinmayi Ma and Shri Naresh Midha, Brisbane, Australia, for sponsoring the entire work; Usha Devi and Siddhartha Krishna for transcribing the original speeches, recorded on audio tapes; Swami Satchidananda, Treasurer of Omkarananda Ashram Himalayas, Rishikesh, for book design and layout; Miss Theresa Clarke "Shanti", Belfast, N. Ireland, and Uddhava Nail Samman, General Secretary of The Traditional Hatha Yoga Association, London, England, for editing and proofreading; Miss Virginia Thorley, OAM, Hon. Secretary, International Lactation Consultant Association (ILCA), Australia, for the final editing and proofreading work; Miss Melissa, Designer, Brisbane, Australia, for designing the cover; and Omkarananda Publishing Department for willingly accepting to publish this work acquainting the readers with the cultural and spiritual heritage of India.

Om Shantih, Shantih, Shantih Om

Prologue

Swami Chinmayi Ma

On 26th October 1932, in the town of Aligarh near Mathura in India, Srimati Rama Devi gave birth to a son. His parents used to call him SuryaPrakash, but he is now known to all of us as Prabhuji. He was born into a Brahmin family (a family of scholastic caste, the highest caste). His father, Sri Prabhupad Acharya Mohan Swarup Shukla, was a great saint and scholar, related to the tradition of Nimbarka (Shukadeva) Sumpradaya. So Prabhuji was educated in "the traditional way" by his father.

At the age of 18 years he left home and went into the Himalayan mountains to the ancient and holy town of Badrinath. He met Swami Sarvanandaji (ji is a term of respect), who was a disciple of the great Vedic scholar Swami Gangeshvaranandan Ji. Prabhuji lived with Swami Gangeshwarananda Ji for several years and studied the Vedas at his holy feet. Swami Ji gave him the name "Suryabhanuh" (He who enlightens the sun).

For another ten years Prabhuji lived in Dehradun furthering his education, with Mahant Sri Indiresh Charan Dasji, from Guru Ramray Darbar. In the meantime he had met a French Mother, Madam Louise Morin, a follower of the great Mahatma Gandhiji, she was at the time caring for Mrs. Indira Gandhi (no relation, and later Prime Minister of India), while her mother passed away in Lausane, Switzerland. Madam Morin had many contacts with great saints and poets of the time, like Rabindranath Tagor, Romio Rollon, and it was at this time that Prabhuji also came into contact with such great statesmen as Pandit Jawaharlal Nehru (The First Prime Minister of India) and Lal Bahadur Shastri. The President of India at the time was Dr. S. Radhakrishnan, who advised Prabhuji to join the Benares Hindu University to do his doctorate degree. This he did. Then he met the great saint Vinoba Bhave, and was inspired by him and the work he was doing – distributing land to the poor, a movement known as Bhudaan, and Prabhuji began working for this cause.

He travelled extensively abroad several times, once travelling overland from Pakistan to France, preaching the essence of the Vedic religion and the message of the great Mahatma Gandhiji of ahimsa, or non-violence. He preached this message in many parts of the world, including many European countries such as France, Belgium, Germany, Switzerland, and England.

In 1973 Prabhuji went into the mountains of the Himalayas again, and this time he lived alone in a cave near Solan, Simla in the state of Himachal Pradesh. Here he did intense tapasya (austerities) until 1979, a period of seven years.

Over the years of his life he came into contact with many great saints and masters in India and abroad. Swami Shivanandaji Maharaj, Swami Vidyananda Giri Ji Maharaj, Swami Venkateshanandaji Maharaj, Swami Muktanandaji Maharaj, Sri Krishnamacharii, J. Krishnamurthy, Ma Anandamayi, Swami Hridayananda Mataji, and many other famous masters and teachers of Yoga.

In his life, he only gave of himself and his knowledge to help those who sought the path of enlightenment. This he continues to do today, in "Krishna Kutir" at Omkarananda Ashram Himalayas, on the banks of the holy river Ganges, in Rishikesh. He is a scholar of many languages, including Sanskrit, English and French.

This book is a compilation of the discourses that Prabhuji delivered in the Samadhi Hall of Gurudev Swami Shivanandaji Maharaj, in the Shivananda Ashram Rishikesh, in the year 1991-1992.

Contents

Introduction 11
Verse 1 15
Verse 2 17
Verse 3 19
Verse 4 25
Verse 5 32
Verse 6 41
Verse 7 49
Verse 8 52
Verse 9 59
Verse 10 66
Verse 11 74
Verse 12 83
Verse 13 85
Verse 14 92
Verse 15 94
Verse 16 102
Verse 17 104
Verse 18 110
Verse 19 118
Verse 20 125
Verse 21 132
Verse 22 139
Verse 23 141
Verse 24 142
Verse 25 148
Verse 26 150

Introduction

The **Bhagavad Gita** is the most beloved scripture of India. It occupies a position next only to the **Upanishads** or to the holy **Veda Bhagavan**. It is considered as a summing up of the **Upanishads**. In **Gita Dhyanam** it is said that all the **Upanishads** are cows, the milker is Sri Krishna, the calf is Arjuna, the enjoyers are the wise ones and the milk is the fine nectar that the **Gita** is. The **Gita** is a constituent of the threefold canon **Prasthanatraya** of Hinduism; the other two being the **Upanishads** and the **Brahmasutras**. The **Srimad Bhagavad-Gita** occurs in the **Bhisma Parva** of the great epic the **Mahabharata** and comprises 18 chapters of which the third one is the chapter of **Karma Yoga**, the Yoga of action. The scene of the delivery of the **Bhagavad Gita**, "The Song Divine", by Sri Krishna and Arjuna is laid on the battlefield of Kuruksetra where the Pandavas and the Kauravas had assembled their armies for war. According to tradition the battle was fought at the end of the Dvaparayuga, before the Kali Yuga has started. Kali Yuga is believed to have started in 3102 B.C., when Pariksita, grandson of Arjuna ascended the throne of the Kauravas at Hastinapura. The teachings of Lord Krishna in spite of being beginningless were lost to the world through a long lapse of time because of the absence of the sages who could impart it. Lord Krishna describes how this ancient Yoga was handed down from ancient times and proves how it existed from time immemorial.

The message of Sri Krishna in the Bhagavad Gita is the perfect answer for the modern age, as well for any age: the Yoga of dutiful action, of non-attachment, for God or

Self-realisation. The path made by Sri Krishna is the golden path for both the busy man who has his duties in the material world and for the highest spiritual aspirant who has renounced the world. This path helps us to fulfil our righteous duties on this earth, it leads us to Self-realisation, to the true Self. Sri Krishna was one of the greatest examples of divinity, because he lived and manifested himself as God, an Avatara, and at the same time performed the duties of a noble king. When Sri Krishna incarnated on earth, Arjuna, a great sage Nara in his previous life, took birth also to be his companion. Great souls always bring with them spiritual associates from past lives to assist them in their present mission.

Vedavyasa, the great Rishi, sage and compiler of all the **Vedas**, **Puranas**, in the **Mahabharata** does not only describe a historical battle on the plain of Kuruksetra in North-India, he also describes a universal battle – the one that rages daily in man's life. This is an important point. Man has to fight innumerable battles in each incarnation right from the moment of conception to the surrender of the last breath. Man has to fight between good and evil, life and death, knowledge and ignorance, health and disease, self-control and temptation, discrimination and blind sense mind. The whole intent of the **Gita** is to align man's effort on the side of Dharma or righteousness.

In the third chapter the discipline of action is described, in which a person – by performing actions for the welfare of others, without any selfish motive – attains equanimity. Bhagavan Sri Krishna says very clearly, "**Na hi kascitksanamapi jatu tisthtyakarmakrt**", no one can ever be without work even for a moment. Can you imagine, without work human civilization would be a jungle of diseases, famine and confusion. It is not necessary to flee the responsibilities of material life. Start by bringing God here where He has placed us, no matter what our environment may be. Surrender all actions to Him, and with the mind concentrated on Him, free from desire and egoism, perform actions. He, Lord Krishna, says clearly, "**Karmanyevadhikaraste ma phalesu kadascana**" — You have a right to action alone, but never at all to its fruit! Perform all your duties being stabilised in Yoga. Devote thyself to Yoga. Yoga is skill in action, "yogah karmasu kausalam", When a man performs actions for himself, it means that he has a desire for the fruit of actions and where there is desire for the fruit of actions, there is the possibility of the performance of forbidden actions. Even a Karma Yogi renders service to the body but does not let the body become sleepy, indolent, heedless, idle and pleasure-seeking. Even he renders service to the senses but does not allow them to be engaged in worldly pleasures. He also renders service to the mind, but does not allow the mind to think of doing harm to others or thinking of sense objects or futile things. He serves the intellect by not allowing it to think of the duties of others. He serves all of them by having neither the feeling of mineness nor attachment.

So the teachings of the **Gita** are based on man's experience. Lord Krishna makes it very clear that the body and the soul are totally different from each other. The body is unreal, limited and perishable, the soul eternal, real, omnipresent and imperishable. That's why we should never feel sad at the time of destruction of the perishable nor should we have a desire to maintain the imperishable. When a human being discriminates the self from the body which is a necessity in all actions and disciplines of Yoga, the desire for liberation is aroused.

Every person deserves God-realisation. The human body has been given to us to realise Him alone. As soon as a man sincerely resolves to attain liberation, God-realisation, his attachment and attractions to the material world begin to disappear. Attachment to pleasure and prosperity are the main hindrances to attaining God-realisation.

Usha Devi

Karma Yoga

(The Art of Working)

Verse 1

अर्जुन उवाच ।
ज्यायसी चेत्कर्मणस्ते मता बुद्धिर्जनार्दन ।
तत्किं कर्मणि घोरे मां नियोजयसि केशव ॥ १ ॥

Arjuna uvāca :
jyāyasī cet-karmaṇas-te matā buddhir-janārdana I
tat-kiṁ karmaṇi ghore māṁ ni-yojayasi keśava II 1 II

Arjuna said:

O Janardana, if you think that knowledge is superior to action, then why, o Kezava, do you engage me in this terrible action?

jyāyasī – superior; cet – if; karmaṇaḥ – to action; te – by thee; matā – considered, thought; buddhiḥ – knowledge, wisdom; janārdana – O Lord Krishna; tat – then; kim – why; karmaṇi – in action; ghore – terrible; mām – me; niyojayasi – engage; keśava – O Lord Krishna.

Arjuna ordered Lord Krishna to place his chariot between the two armies so that he could observe the warriors eager for battle. When Lord Krishna has placed the chariot in between, in front of Bhisma and Drona and the other kings, delusion in Arjuna was aroused, he was deluded, because of his attachment to his kinsmen. So, Arjuna thought knowledge to be superior to action as, in the case of knowledge, a man does not have to perform such horrible deeds as slaughter in war. That's why Arjuna posed this question in front of Bhagavan Sri Krishna. "Then if it is so, why do You engage me in this frightful work?"

Arjuna was confused and deluded at that time. He misunderstood the teaching of Sri Krishna. Sri Krishna taught Arjuna in the second chapter, verse 49, concerning the wisdom of **Sankhya Yoga**, that "action is far inferior to the discipline of knowledge". But now in the third chapter Lord Krishna is teaching Arjuna the wisdom concerning **Karma Yoga,** the discipline of action.

Undoubtedly, bodily activities are indeed inferior to the knowledge of the Self. Until the delusion of the body is conquered, a man is totally unable to manifest wisdom. To destroy the false identity with the body, man has to engage in "the inferior, yet necessary, liberating outer activities". Employing action to attain inaction is illustrated in the Vedic scriptures as using a thorn to remove another thorn. Once the seeker has rid himself of the delusion of the body consciousness, he is automatically freed from the necessity for action. Neither the body nor its activities have any further value; they have served the purpose for which they were created and the seeker is ripe for the manifestation of wisdom. In the highest state of consciousness all activities are transcended.

Verse 2

व्यामिश्रेणेव वाक्येन बुद्धिं मोहयसीव मे ।
तदेकं वद निश्चित्य येन श्रेयोऽहमाप्नुयाम् ॥ २ ॥

Vyāmiśreṇeva vākyena buddhiṁ mohayasīva me I
tadekaṁ vada niścitya yena śreyo'ham-āpnuyām II 2 II

> *By these apparently conflicting words, you seem to confuse my understanding. Tell me that one path for certain by which I can attain to the highest good.*

vyāmiśreṇa iva – by that seemingly or apparently conflicting, perplexing; vākyena – with words, statement, with speech; buddhim – understanding; mohayasi – art bewildering, confusing; iva – as it were; me – my; tat ekam – that one (either knowledge or action); vada – tell; niścitya – for certain; yena – by which; śreyaḥ – highest good; aham – I; āpnuyām – shall attain.

Arjuna is confused, although it is not the intention of Sri Krishna to confuse Arjuna. In this confusion Arjuna is not able to understand whether he should perform his duty or take refuge in intellect. We can understand his confusion, because different paths like **Sankhya Yoga** or **Karma Yoga** were explained in the previous verses. In the second chapter, verse 31, it has been clearly stated, that "There is no greater good fortune for a Kshatriya then a righteous war". In the same chapter in verse 48 and 49, Lord Krishna asked Arjuna to perform his duty, while sometimes He asks him to seek refuge in intellect.

Arjuna wants to clear up this apparently confusing matter so that any common man could accept **Karma Yoga** and **Jnana Yoga** without misinterpretation.

He requested Lord Krishna to tell him clearly by which principle, either of action or of knowledge, he may attain the highest good. Arjuna is asking for a clear, single path by which the human intelligence can move straight to the supreme good.

Verse 3

श्रीभगवानुवाच ।
लोकेऽस्मिन्द्विविधा निष्ठा पुरा प्रोक्ता मयाऽनघ ।
ज्ञानयोगेन संख्यानां कर्मयोगेन योगिनाम् ॥ ३ ॥

Sri Bhagavān-uvāca :
loke'smin-dvividhā niṣṭhā purā proktā mayā'nagha I
jñāna-yogena saṅkhyānāṁ karma-yogena yogināṁ II 3 II

The blessed Lord said:

O blameless One, in this world a two-fold way of life has been taught of yore by Me, the path of knowledge for men of contemplation and that of work for men of action.

Sri Bhagavan – the blessed Lord; uvāca – said; loke'smin – in this world, in this world for the people of the three castes who were qualified for following the scriptures; dvividhā – twofold; niṣṭhā – path, steadfastness, persistence in what is undertaken; purā – previously, in the beginning, in the days of yore, in the beginning of creation; proktā – said, were spoken of; mayā – by me; anagha – o sinless one, unblemished one; jñānayogena – by the path of knowledge; sāṅkhyānām – of the saṅkhyās, of the meditative; karmayogena – by the path of action; yoginām – of the Yogis, of the active, the men of action (rites and duties).

The integral life of an individual consists of **Karma Yoga, Bhakti Yoga** and **Jnana Yoga**. Every individual has a head, a heart and two hands. The head corresponds to

Jnana Yoga (The Yoga of Knowledge), the heart to **Bhakti Yoga** (The Yoga of Devotion) and the hands to **Karma Yoga** (The Yoga of Action). If we want to realise God, then all these three are required, otherwise if one of them is missing, the personality becomes lopsided. For integral evolution of an individual all three are necessary. It is not that one person is made for **Jnana Yoga,** another one for **Bhakti Yoga** and another for **Karma Yoga**. No – everybody has a head, a heart and hands! Of course, some people are predominantly intellectual so they may prefer *Jnana Yoga*; some may be more inclined towards devotion and therefore may prefer **Bhakti Yoga**; and others may have preferences towards selfless service and prefer **Karma Yoga.** When these three Yogas evolve in an individual he or she becomes a fully fledged personality. Otherwise there is always something missing in our life.

The great saints, Rishis (Seers) and Yogis have thrown light on all the aspects of our life. They have pondered, reflected, meditated upon what is life, what is its purpose, what is its highest goal. There is hardly any aspect of life which has not been explained or described in our Vedic literature. According to Vedic culture our life has been classified into four **Ashramas,** namely: **Brahmacharya, Grihastha, Vānaprastha and Sannyāsa**. Each **Ashrama** is traditionally said to last 25 years. At the age of 8 years a Brahmin boy is initiated by means of a sacred thread ceremony into the Vedic way of living. As a **Brahmachari** he studies at the feet of his master the sacred scriptures and philosophy and in this way he is prepared for the next **Ashrama – Grihastha** (the life of a householder). On this Ashrama the other three depend for support. The **Grihastha** Asrama was not a licence for a life of lust and passion – self discipline is required. The physical act is meant for creating life. In this **Ashrama** the person evolved into maturity.

Whilst discharging the responsibilities of family life towards wife and children, a man continued to study the scriptures in preparation for the Ashrama to come – **Vānaprastha,** forest life. The forest life was not a primitive life in our Vedic culture. It was not a hindrance in our spiritual development, it was a great help. The great works of the **Upanishads** and **Aranyakas** were composed in forests and woods. So, as the **Grihastha** Ashrama was a preparation for **Vanaprastha**, so **Vanaprastha** was a preparation for the **Sannyasa** Ashrama (renunciation). To be a **Sannyāsi** is not an easy thing – a lot of knowledge, contemplation and thinking is required for real renunciation. Of course, each of the Ashramas was free – if there was **vairagya** (detachment) and renunciation, then even a **Brahmachari** could go directly to **Sannyasa**, but they were few who could do that. According to tradition, a person moved from one Ashrama to the next in consultation with the master and the parents. This is but a brief look into our great Vedic tradition to aid your understanding.

Lokesmin-dvividhā niṣthā - In this world from the beginning of creation, two paths have been given to us for Self-realisation. One is the path of knowledge for men of contemplation – at the mere vision of truth their souls become united with the Supreme Self. The other is the path of action and those God-seekers who take themselves to it reach Divine Truth. Both these paths appear different but are in fact one and the same. The Pure Self can be realised through both paths; it depends upon the innate constitution whether a person is eligible for **Karma** or **Jnana Yoga**.

The divine, spiritual life is very deep. You can never find the real pearls on the surface. They are only found in the depths of an ocean. When the mother-pearl is ready to receive a pearl, she floats with her opened wings on the surface of the ocean. When the star **Svati-naksatra** arises on the horizon and a drop of water falls into her open shell she closes it and descends deep into the ocean. When the pearl is ripened, again she opens, and the pearl falls onto the ocean floor. See how pearls are created in the depths of the ocean! In the same way, in the depth of our mind, the depth of our Self, realisation takes place. Life without realisation is unfulfilled. Until and unless the Self is realised in all human beings, in all creatures, the human being is imperfect. To realise the Self in all beings means to have cosmic divine consciousness. We are born for Self-realisation, sooner or later. If not in this life, then in the next one we are supposed to realise the Self. When Self is realised, great relaxation, peace, harmony takes place in life.

Tarati śokam-ātmavit (Chāndogyopaniṣad - 7/1/3) – if one wants to cross the ocean of sadness and sorrow one has to realise the Self. There is hardly anyone who does not suffer in this world. In ignorance we are born several times. When we realise the difficulties of life, when we suffer a lot in this world, then we do not want to be born again and again. To be born means to suffer. Without suffering there is no birth, there is no creation, nor maintenance of the sustenance of creation. Lord Buddha says that life is full of suffering, and desires are the source of all suffering. When our desires have come to a conclusion, and we have really realised that all desires are the cause of all suffering, then a very strong desire for Self-realisation, for Self-liberation, for the emancipation of the soul, dawns upon us. Many people make an effort for liberty but few people struggle for liberation **(Mokṣa)**. When liberation comes then liberty itself is attained. For liberty we do not have to work, liberty will come by itself.

Why are we studying the **Bhagavad Gita**? Why, in order to enlighten our own Self! We want to realise our Self in the given circumstances, where we are. We are groping so much in darkness, having eyes we do not see with, having ears we do not hear with. We are running from one place to another just escaping our own Self. Without facing our own Self there is no other way out. We can go on escaping our Self but Self will never escape us. Wherever we shall go Self will follow us. How difficult it is to realise and to face one's own Self! See how difficult it is sometimes to sit quietly for five minutes! It is so difficult that we want to escape. As soon as the oil lamp is kindled darkness disappears and you can see all the objects around. Do not think that the darkness in this world will be removed by running around, by fighting, by quarrelling. Darkness of ignorance can only be removed through the light of knowledge or Self-realisation.

Lord Krishna told the same thing to Arjuna. Arjuna was still not ready for the path of **Jnana Yoga**. You move on the path of **Karma Yoga** first, and through **Karma Yoga** your mind and heart will be purified. Until and unless the heart is purified, and mind transparently clear, Self-enlightenment cannot take place. As long as there is dust on the mirror, how shall we be able to see the face clearly? As soon as the dust is removed the reflection is there. We shall see the Self face to face.

Ātmanam viddhi – know thyself, realise thyself. How to realise the Self? Start where you are just now. You have not been placed in the present circumstances meaninglessly, everything is pre-planned. You have to discharge your duty to the best of your ability, just at this moment, wherever you are. We want all the time to become something, we are never satisfied with what we are. Try to be satisfied with what has been given to you. Nobody in this world is self-contented. All the time we want to become something! That is why there are so many conflicts, so much suffering. In the Pure Self there is no becoming – that is the beauty of the Self. When we identify with the Self, when we are aware of the Self, we drink the nectar of peace, devotion, love and affection. These are the spiritual treasures which have been given to us all since we were born. **Uttisṭhata jāgrata prāpya varānnibodhata, Kṣurasya dhārā niṣitā duratyayā durgam pathastat kavayo vadanti** (**Kaṭhopanisad** 1/3/14), "Stand! Arise! Having attained the great masters, realise thy Self! The great seers say the spiritual path is the path of a double-edged razor." If we are not careful we are just cut into two pieces. The more we grow on this path, the more difficulties and problems will appear on this path. That is why the great saints are warning us to wake up. Consciously or unconsciously everybody tries in their own way to realise the Self, even through this material evolution which is also made for our Self-realisation. This is a fact which is mostly not understood.

Verse 4

न कर्मणामनारम्भान्नैष्कर्म्यं पुरुषोऽश्नुते ।
न च संन्यसनादेव सिद्धिं समधिगच्छति ॥ ४ ॥

Na karmaṇām-anārambhān-naiṣkarmyaṁ puruṣo'śnute I
na ca sannyasanād-eva siddhiṁ samadhigacchati II 4 II

Not by abstention from work does a man attain freedom from action; nor by mere renunciation does he attain to his perfection.

Na – not; karmaṇām – of actions, of works; anārambhāt – from non-performance, by abstaining; naiṣkarmyam – actionlessness, worklessness; purusaḥ – man, a person; aśnute – reaches; ca – and; sannyasanāt – from renunciation, from giving up; eva – only, merely; siddhim – perfection; samadhigacchati – attains.

That which we do – actions, are called **karma** in Sanskrit. Man performs not only one action but many during the day, during an entire lifetime! This talking, for example, is action. The mind vibrates and we think, and thinking is an activity alert with awareness. The mind thinks and it is only an active mind which can think. **Karmanam** means many actions and is a specific term in Vedic literature. Those Vedic actions like **Yajna** (**yaj** is the root, which means to worship, to adore), and those works which are done in the adoration of the Divine, are called **yajna**. **Yajna** are not all the actions we do in our lifetime but are the specific actions, the worshipping deeds, which are done in the spirit of, the attitude of, worship of the divine. That means only those actions in which our attitude changes are the actions done in Divine Consciousness. When the consciousness changes then the action becomes a **yajna**. Worship involves sacrifice, because self, which means ego, is sacrificed. We can only worship God when there is sacrifice of our ego. God lives in all, so when actions are done for the welfare of all, then we do not do them from the egoistic point of view. We try to eliminate our ego or, so to say, merge it in the Divine. It is this merging of the ego in the Divine that we should understand, rather than its elimination or sacrifice. We should try to understand, too, the real significance, the purpose of **yajna**.

Yajna are selfless actions in which self is sacrificed. Some deeds are done with ego – with pride and arrogance – and these are not **yajna**. **Yajna** are actions which are not done in pride, arrogance, hatred, which are not forced, not imposed, which are spontaneous, are free of the self – the ego. You just do them, just slip into meditation. Slowly, slowly, you land in meditation. It is the need of an individual; our consciousness, our mind, needs peace of mind immediately. Everybody needs it, but people are not usually aware so they do not meditate. Those who are aware meditate, they give peace to the mind. As in sleep we give rest to our body, in the same way we give rest also in our meditations. So you do it very spontaneously, voluntarily.

So, **naiskarmyam** is what action done selflessly, or in the devotional spirit, or with offering to the Divine, is called. It is the state where one is unaffected by work. This disposition or state of mind is attained while doing selfless actions – actions free from desire for the fruits of such actions. **Bhava** is a word which means a state of being (**bhu** is a root which means to become, to manifest). When we do a particular kind of action, our state of being also becomes according to that action. While doing the action we do not feel that we are acting because Self, the **Atman**, does not act. The **Atman** is devoid of action being all-pervasive and all-pervading. The **Atman** is balanced, in equilibrium, in an equipoised state of consciousness. It is only our mind which is unbalanced but Self is always balanced – that is why, we adjust our mind according to It. And the mind also becomes balanced when we are Self-established. That is why we sit in meditation, because in meditation Self-awareness comes, and with that comes the equipoised state of mind. Many problems are created in our lives because we are unbalanced in our minds, *not* in our Self which is always balanced. Just as the sky is balanced – only the clouds are unbalanced. On the surface of the ocean when waves are created there is movement, unbalance, but on the horizon where the sky and ocean meet, there is peace, as if it is balanced. So, the sky is peaceful, and the depths of the ocean are also quiet; on the surface alone there are ripples, tides and typhoons.

So, also in the deeper state of our consciousness there is eternal peace, fathomless peace, but we do not identify ourselves with that Self. We identify with the ripples and as the ripples are moved we also become moved and we begin to think that we are disturbed. That 'i' (self) is disturbed though 'I' (Self) is not disturbed. 'I' cannot be disturbed, nothing can disturb 'Me', 'You'. It is only the mind which is disturbed, some sentiments, or sensations, are disturbed. Disturbance takes place only on the surface of our individuality, our personality. In the deeper core of your personality, in the deeper state of your consciousness you remain always unperturbed. But you do not discover it, become aware of it. When we sit together and meditate, in that you discover (which means uncover) that which was covered, just as in the middle of ash the spark is there, but you have to remove the layers of ash to see it. In the same way that the divine spark is there, a deep peace – the eternal ocean of peace – is flowing, and we are not aware of it! So you begin to think that you are disturbed, that you lose your temper. And it so happens that after you lose your temper you become quiet and you forget it. It just comes, not only to you but to highly evolved souls also – they lose their temper, become angry, restless and unquiet. Even the ocean too! Just see – if there are waves and ripples in a pond you will not be surprised because it is a limited body of water. If there are ripples on the river Ganges you will not be surprised because however mighty it is, **it is** a river, and in flood sometimes. And not only that, even the great oceans have tides with the waxing and waning of the moon.

So, relatively speaking, there is a movement on one extreme of our individuality and personality, otherwise life would become impossible. If there would be no activity, no movement, then life would not be able to exist. For that purpose all the different moods are needed but at the same time, in the midst of it all, there is another extreme of yourself which remains completely untouched, unperturbed, quiet, restful, peaceful – eternally in peace. Clouds come and go but the sky remains unchanged. The sun is never absent – only our vision is curtailed by clouds or the position of our planet. In the same way, our Self is never absent, Pure Self always remains. That is the beauty of the Self – It eternally IS! Its eternal presence is there and is realised in the moment of meditation, in samādhi. So it is this consciousness which has been praised and manipulated in this beautiful verse. If a person does not do the action, if – due to some lethargic state of mind, of body, because of **tamas** – he doesn't perform deeds, then he doesn't attain the state of actionlessness. He doesn't become aware that the Self is actionless. Self is actionless, it is **body** which is performing deeds and actions.

So, if a person says, 'I will attain Self-awareness merely by not doing deeds, let me not perform actions. I will close my eyes and sit in meditation for a long time', that will not be possible, because activity is a necessity of a human. After some time you will be tired and again the urges will come, a state of activity will rise in you and force you to do actions. You will not be able to live for long without doing actions – actions are also equally in your nature. So, we may not perform actions because we are lazy, sleepy or intoxicated, but that is not the state of actionlessness. The real state of actionlessness is the state of the Self, Self-awareness. As soon as the state of Self-awareness comes, you become quiet. Even in the midst of anger, if somehow or another Self-awareness comes, the anger will disappear. At that time you do not identify yourself with anger, you identify with the Pure Self-awareness – you become **THAT** at that time. But if I identify so much with anger I **become** anger. Some people who are Self-aware have anger but immediately they control it and govern it, and it disappears as soon as Self-awareness comes, because Self by itself is quiet, serene.

In our daily life we are often hectic and forget that we are Self. That is why **satsang** is so important. In **satsang** we try to be Self-established. The atmosphere is such that we meditate and attain peace of mind. Let anyone who comes from outside and who is angry sit for a moment in meditation and he will become quiet. Mind will be attuned, in harmony. This state of harmony, in tune with infinity, is not attained merely by not doing actions. In the name of religion, in the name of **sannyasa**, there are many people who are not doing actions. Those who are not doing actions, are they really purely Self-aware? No, they are ignorant. So, if through ignorance one does not do actions then it is laziness, it is the state devoid of action. It is a negative state. Self-awareness is a positive state of Realisation, eternally in peace, silence and quietude. And it can also be while you are doing your action, and sometimes even more when you are not doing action. How beautiful is life when it is realised and experienced, and it is this that has been emphasized in this verse. But we have to be sensitive to it, and if we are, then our whole life becomes love. Love then appears in our life in the true sense of the term. There are thousands of shades and nuances of love and if they are not realised then how can you create a picture of your life? In order to create a beautiful picture of your life, work in the way a lover works for his beloved – in great joyous love, Love has assumed the form of an action – the whole of your life becomes filled with joy and happiness. Love is a blissful cup, and it is this cup of love which Bhagavan Sri Krishna is asking the devotee to drink. Taste and drink! Let your love flow like the Ganges, ceaselessly, day and night, in all seasons. Then you become divine in the core of your nature. The mind becomes quiet.

When activity is done in love it is not a burden. This talk with you is not a burden. This hour spent together talking may raise a question: is the rest of the 23 hours in our daily life like this? Life must be like this! This is only a token of love which is given to you. Let the other hours become like this conversation, this **satsang**. **Sat** means truth, **sanga** means communion – communion with truth and truth is God. During this hour we become one with the Divine, with the real existence of the Divine. The Divine Existence comes to us, we begin to exist divinely in our life. The rest of the time we were not divinely existing, we were not conscious of the Divine Existence. The whole **problem** of life is this! So our life becomes a burden. But if our whole life becomes divine who wouldn't like to live it – great souls are trying for that! You do not become

Swami Sivananda, Anandamayee Ma or St. Francis of Assisi, or Christ, in one day! So, when this state of consciousness appears, when the sun of Love dawns upon you, then life is really full. And it is for this you are born. If birth is given consciously for this then even to take birth is worthwhile. That's why devotees in India say, "O my Lord, I would not mind being born but all I expect from Thee is that I may not forget Thee." See how beautiful! Christ said, "I and My Father are One" – one with His heart. Christ became one with the Divine, He was doing divine activity and His whole life was a continuous prayer. He did not need to go to a church. At the seashore, by the river He was in the continuous companionship of the Divine. In such a way we are really required to realise and if we realise this life, it is perfect, a joy and peace.

Verse 5

न हि कश्चित्क्षणमपि जातु तिष्ठत्यकर्मकृत् ।
कार्यते ह्यवशः कर्म सर्वः प्रकृतिजैर्गुणैः ॥ ५ ॥

Na hi kaścit-kṣaṇam-api jātu tiṣṭhaty-akarmakṛt I
kāryate hy-avaśaḥ karma sarvaḥ prakṛtijair-guṇaiḥ II 5 II

For no one can remain even for a moment without doing work; everyone is made to act helplessly by the impulses born out of nature.

Na hi – not verily; kaścit – any one; kṣaṇam – a moment, for an instant; api – even; jātu – verily, ever; tiṣṭhati – remains, rests; akarmakṛt – without performing action, without doing work; kāryate – is made to do; hi – for; avaśaḥ – helpless, under compulsion; karma – action; sarvaḥ – all, all creatures; prakṛtijaiḥ – born of Prakrti; guṇaiḥ – by the qualities, by the three Gunas.

Prakriti is composed of **sattva** (the quality of knowledge), **rajas** (the quality of action) and **tamas** (the quality of inertia). Nature is made out of these three elements – **sattva, rajas** and **tamas**. These three constituent parts oblige the individual to do work, that is why no one will be able to live without work even for a moment. For example, I am talking and as you are sitting, listening, ideas will come and ideas are the function of our brain. It is a very subtle activity, but activity which is an expression of a subtle thought; activity which is a vibration and where there is a vibration there is an action. So, it is hardly possible that a person can be without doing work even if it is not work with his hands. Sometimes people are sitting on a chair, moving their legs or writing something without knowing, unconsciously. It is in the nature of man to do something – even a small child cannot sit without doing something, and so also with adults. In an advanced civilization people are supposed to work. Human nature has been studied very deeply and it was seen that people would not be able to do without work. And if it is not right work it cannot be **sattvic** work – they will be doing **rajasic** work. And if not **rajasic** then it will be **tamasic** – they will hate, be envious, they will be ill. We see all kinds of things in society as the result of the interaction and action of these three constituent elements which are part of **prakriti**. Every human being is subjected to these three constituent parts, which is very important to note, because we are our body, mind and thinking; all this is made out of **prakriti.** If a man cannot live without doing work it is not his fault. It is because he is made out of **prakriti** and **prakriti** obliges him to do so – there is an energy and this energy has to exhaust itself. In some people there is a lot of energy and they do lots of work; in others there is less and they do less work; and there are people who are very refined and their activities will be related to writing, dance, painting, music, and the sciences. All of these are due to the activities of the **gunas** (**sattva, rajas, tamas**) of **prakriti**.

Prakriti is often translated as nature in the sense of trees growing, flowers blooming, rivers flowing, sun rising – quiet and silent activities in nature. But the real significance of **prakriti** is different. **Prakriti** is equilibrium of the three **gunas** (qualities). **Prakriti** is like a rope and the gunas are like its strands. In Sanskrit **guna** also means 'a strand'. A rope is made by taking three strands and twisting them together. So out of three one is made, the rope itself. In the same way this **prakriti** consists out of the three **gunas** (qualities). So **Prakriti** is like a rope.

Human beings are tied by this rope of *prakriti*, tied by the rope of their nature – this **prakriti**, of the three **gunas**. Man has tried to dominate all creatures in the world including the lion which is such a fearless animal in the forest. He is also caged and controlled, and what about the elephant and others? And man also tries to dominate man, to control and govern, but there is something very curious in a human being's nature that he does not want to be governed. By nature he does not like an authoritarian attitude – he doesn't want there to be any authority over him. Why? Because there is already an authority of nature that controls and governs him, his soul for example. He has already taken on the abiding nature of this **prakriti** – it governs him because of these three elements, these constituent parts, **sattva**, **rajas** and **tamas**. If the life of a human being is governed by another then he does not like it and he retaliates.

We should try to understand human nature. Bhagavan Sri Krishna is also saying this in this verse, **na hi kaścit-kṣaṇam-api**, which means "even for a moment we cannot live without doing activity". It is **nature** which governs man to do work, which obliges and forces him to do so. Even if he is left alone, immediately he will do something. Incessant activity is the call of nature, the call of **prakriti**. The sages observed the natural phenomenon which exists in the world of creation, and with the help of this phenomenon tried to explain the numen which is beyond nature, and which is in everybody. What about the numen, what about this self, this soul? Why? Because it wants to liberate all the bondage of **prakriti** in us. The self retaliates, it does not want to be governed at all, it does not accept any kind of governance. It just wants to be one with all – that is human nature. To transcend the three **gunas** is a very deep urge in the human mind, in human nature.

According to the Yoga **Sutras** very great souls who have entered into **nirvikalpa samadhi** or **nirbija samadhi** are in a highly thought-free state. They can be said to have transcended the three **gunas** and they are free, they are in liberation, they may not work. But before that stage, everybody has to do work, and must work otherwise we'll fall down – we will fall down if we do not go up. If there is no effort to go up then the fall is certain – down is there. So either we must climb, we must transcend these three elements, and it is with the help of the Self – ingrained in every human being – that we can transcend this nature, **prakriti**, these three constituent parts of **prakriti**. All action that you are seeing is taking place in **prakriti**, it is not taking place in the Self. Self is motionless – peaceful, calm, quiet, serene like the depth of the ocean. Activities are just ripples on the surface in **prakriti**. When **Purusa** who is the sole Self, identifies Himself with **prakriti** we used to think that He was an actor! Self is not an actor! He lives completely in serenity and peace, and that is why we meditate, because in meditation we realise our nature of peace and tranquillity. Everybody!

When this call to meditate comes from within, this clarion call from the depths, from the bottom of the heart, **then** it is a sincere meditation. Otherwise in meditation all kinds of imaginations, fears, suspicions, doubts, and emotions come. Is this meditation? No, this is not meditation, it is an entirely different thing. That is why we move very slowly on the path of meditation until we attain the right state. It is a state of consciousness which comes to everybody at the right time, and the right way.

Bhagavan Sri Krishna says, it is the law of nature which will oblige you, force you to work. That is why if you decide to sit for a long time in your closed room you will find that you'll run away, you will want to see the world outside. Great souls, Yogis, saints and sages, when they retire and go into meditation it is after a very great effort. They make a Herculean effort when they go into themselves, and they try to disclose the mystery that is taking place inside their own Self, and in the environment outside. Then they have transcended nature and not otherwise. Arjuna was retreating from action not knowing that his nature would force him to act. Do you know what happens in a person who has a quarrelsome nature? He will pick quarrels everywhere. He will quarrel even with himself, with animals, with brutes, with trees in the forest. A warrior is quarrelsome by nature and if not engaged in war will find other things to quarrel over – some nations find this more so than others! The instinct of anger is there. So, the thing is, we have to soften this instinct which is made of the constituent part of nature, understand and transcend it. And how nicely the **Gita** is taking us on the spiritual path so that we may really attain the Divine Life!

The Divine Path is not attained in one day, or by eating some drug, or by living wonderful imaginations. Not living the right kind of life, the real rational way of life, and taking various substances leads to all kinds of problems for individuals and society. Lives are wasted and some end in suicide. These people said, "Why should we meditate, we can just take drugs and be in silence and peace." If it was so easy to realise the Self then everyone would take drugs! Great saints followed the right process, right way of doing. They did not artificially create any kind of consciousness, as consciousness is an evolution. And how can this be evolved? The technique has been nicely given in the **Gita**, and slowly, slowly, if you really understand the **Bhagavad Gita** your life becomes divine, you become filled with joy, all your problems are solved, you become normal – all abnormalities disappear. All mental problems disappear.

How many mental problems are created in the western world? They have come this way because our people want to experience the same advancement of civilization! Please don't think that I am criticizing the material evolution. It is needed for our Self-realisation. Please try to understand. We cannot cut ourselves off from the noble traditions of the past – we are the outcome of traditions.

This river, the Ganges, flowing in front of us, comes from the high snow-covered peaks of the Himalayan mountains many kilometres away. And how is it that you can cut off from the whole origin of the river? People go to Gangotri for example, to see the source of Ganga and all the way there the cold, clean, fresh, nectar-like Ganga water is flowing. The noble traditions are like the river flowing in ourselves. If we cut off from the noble traditions without understanding them, we are the losers. We lose something very important, and we become like a rootless tree. Tell me, how long will a tree survive without roots? If you pull off some leaves, some branches, then of course the tree will survive, but how will it survive in the absence of roots?

So, these noble traditions we are studying here are the roots of our own self. In the absence of the roots the tree will wither away, it will collapse and fall down, it will be dry and dead. We humans hang onto this civilization which has so many problems, but at the same time it is in the midst of this civilization that we should try and uplift ourselves to the noble traditions of the past. Be aware that everything that is from the past is not necessarily bad, nor is it necessarily good because it comes from the past. It should be tested with our reason and experience. And everything that is new, because it is new, is also not necessarily good. So, good or bad, right or wrong, we should try to select, and selection must be there with understanding. Buddha emphasized this to his disciples by preaching: "Please don't accept this because it is coming from me. If it appeals to your reason you accept it, if it does not you return it to me." His approach was rational and people embraced it 2500 years ago. A great revolution in the Indian mind was created by his freshness. But many people, traditional and orthodox, did not like his approach and criticized and abused him bitterly. Buddha was fearless – he stood up and gave the message of compassion and love with all love. The greatest thing is love – there is nothing greater than love and compassion. When any teaching is combined with love and compassion then it goes very deeply into society, into the souls of mankind. Buddha meditated and came out of it like a river, and flowed through society.

We are living in the modern world, in society, and we are facing difficulties. How to face them? We are subjected to confusion and conflict, sometimes we want to take part, sometimes we don't. So, Bhagavan Sri Krishna says to Arjuna: "If you want to escape from discharging the duty of your life do you think that you will be able to resolve the problems? If you will not fight on the war-front then you will fight inside the monastery!" And this happens – people who come from the warrior or aristocratic families fight inside the Ashrams. They create wars and battles, Ashram between Ashram. Envy and jealousy, all these instincts infest these people. Why? Because nature is there at work! They have not gone through the right process. The right process would have been to eliminate these things first – the functions, expressions, manifestations of nature. Then he or she can become a real **Sannyasi** and render a great service to the whole world. But these ills were not removed and somehow they put on a orange robe. Do you think that such a robe makes one a **Sannyasi** (monk) or

Sadhu (saint)? The robe does not make a man, it is the inner transformation, the mind, the outlook, the attitude towards life that makes him or her a saint or a **Sadhu**, or a monk or a **Sannyasi**.

"**Kāryate hy-avaśah karma**" – **Kāryate** means he is **made** to do something, *forced* to, he is **obliged** to do something, in spite of himself. Even if he resists, his nature will force him to do something. That stands for Arjuna. Arjuna has not exercised his active nature so how can he renounce the world and put on saffron coloured dress, shave his head, and pretend that he has become a **Sannyasi** overnight? That is what happens sometimes in many ashrams. Then what is the use of **Sadhana**, of thinking, of studying the scriptures, of meditation? We have to wait for evolution until it takes place at the right time. Now the mango season is coming, there will be blossoms on the trees, bees will be busy – such activity for fertilization! And then the mangoes will come. There will be rain, and scorching heat from the sun and the mangoes will be ripe and sweet with nectar-like juice. See!

So, nature is also working on the mind and heart, and it is this work that Bhagavan Sri Krishna is teaching his devotees: "Look here, you can't resist it, your nature will oblige you, If you run away out of guilt, reaction, terror, compassion, love, the relief will last only a moment, your nature will come back and you will do exactly what your nature dictates." Nature is a great dictator and dictates every movement that governs the ordinary soul. A great soul like Krishna or Buddha or Christ governs nature. In this case the soul governs nature. The ordinary man is moved by the impulses of nature, he is the slave of his hatred, anger and jealousy, he is not the master. But a real developed and evolved soul of the **Bhagavad Gita**, of Yoga, is the one who is the master. He guides the destiny of the impulses, he himself is not guided. An ordinary person, a weaker soul, is guided by nature. Nature is supposed to be dominated and when it is that person is supposed to be called **Swami.** But everyone is a slave of himself, of ego, pride, anger, hatred, and chance. This is the action which is taking place and if you will not obey the higher action on the higher plane then you have to obey the law of nature but on the lower plane, the inferior plane, and become the plaything of hatred, anger, jealousy, malaise, gossip. **Prakriti** means the inferior nature and until you have eliminated the lower planes, lower layers of your consciousness, how will you see the path within? This path is covered by the layers of consciousness and the layer we are discussing is called **Prakriti.** When it is gone, then you can have clear vision of this inner path out of which Self-realisation comes.

This is the work of the **Bhagavad Gita**, that inner revolution, the inner attitude, the inner Self-realisation. If such work could be done in our society, how smooth it will be and how fast it will change! People are trying to remove the darkness with bombs and guns. Do you think they will be able to do it? Darkness cannot be removed by closing it in a suitcase and throwing it in Ganga. It is the aim of the **Bhagavad Gita** to dispel ignorance and darkness. Arjuna says he is helpless – what to do? He is in the bondage of **prakriti** – nature. He is in the bondage of these three constituent elements, bourn out of nature – **sattva**, **rajas** and **tamas**. How to transcend them will be spoken of further.

Verse 6

कर्मेन्द्रियाणि संयम्य य आस्ते मनसा स्मरन्।
इन्द्रियार्थान्विमूढात्मा मिथ्याचारः स उच्यते ॥ ६ ॥

Karmendriyāṇi saṁyamya ya āste manasā smaran I
indriyārthān-vimūḍhātmā mithyācāraḥ sa ucyate II 6 II

He who restrain his organs of action but continues in his mind to brood over the organs of sense, whose nature is deluded, is said to be a hypocrite.

karmendriyāṇi – organs of action, hands, etc,; saṁyamya – restraining, after withdrawing; yaḥ – who; āste – sits; manasā – by the mind, mentally; smaran – remembering, recollecting, thinking; indriyārthān – sense objects; vimūḍhātmā – person having deluded understanding, or deluded mind; mithyācāraḥ – hypocrite; saḥ – he, that one; ucyate – is called.

Karmendriyāṇi means the organs of action, and they are five: the organs of generation, of excretion, the hands, the feet and the tongue. Without a tongue I would not be able to talk – it includes the vocal cords which have to vibrate, to move, and only then speech comes. We have to make an effort, in fact we have to use great energy in order to talk. There are some people who want to remain silent because a lot of energy is spent in cruel and useless conversations and gossiping. The energy is there – so either they are criticizing someone or unnecessarily speaking evil of others, or using ill words. They are not properly using the energy because they are not aware of it. They have not disciplined their tongues. There are so many beautiful things with which the tongue can be occupied. So, there are five **Karmendriyas**, and also five **jnanendriyas** – senses of perception which are: hearing, touch, sight, taste and smell. Bhagavan Sri Krishna says, "**Karmendriyāṇi saṁyamya**" – he who has controlled the organs of action. A person who has only outwardly controlled the organs of action out of fear, laziness, or because he doesn't want to use his hands, considers work with his hands beneath his dignity. He also does not want to use his feet. "**Karmendriyāṇi saṁyamya ya āste manasā smaran**" – the one who has controlled his organs of action but sits quietly without doing anything. But sitting thinks about the sense objects; **indriyārthān** — means the objects of sense perception to which he is always attracted from inside. Even if the eyes are closed he likes to see, if he has closed his ears he likes to hear. Even if he has closed his tongue he likes to taste nice dishes! He has withdrawn from outside his sense of perception and also the organs of action. But from inside, through his mind, he is thinking about the objects of the senses. In thinking about them, then naturally he is attracted to them and the mind cannot be quiet. So he has only controlled the organs of action from outside but has not controlled the mind.

All the senses of perception are important because without them we will not know what the world is. You will ask, should we not enjoy the world – what is the world, why are the sense objects given to us? Does Bhagavan mean that we should not experience the world? No, not at all – use the experience received through the sense objects but don't be infatuated, hypnotized by them. **Vimudhatma** is a word for one who is caught up in the sense perceptions, whose mind is infatuated. He lives in the world and is hypnotized by the sense objects, and has lost the sense of identification with something. **Mudhatma** means an ordinary infatuated person, **vimudhatma** means one who is specially, greatly infatuated, very much involved in the sensuous pleasures of life. When we are hypnotized like this the sensuous world becomes the cause of our bondage. We are not a witness. If attachment, infatuation is not there you are a pure witness. Just like the river is flowing – it is not attached to the banks. If the river was attached to the banks it would not flow. It would become a pond and become dirty. So if your flow is not stopped then you are not attached. Attachment stops your activity; you are blocked, and your growth is marred. You don't grow properly in attachment, flow is not there, vision is not clear – it is coloured. So also our thinking. We are born to liberate, not bind ourselves. If we are not masters of the sense objects then we are their slaves, and such bondage or imprisonment is painful and it does not help anyone to evolve to liberation and freedom.

Ya āste manasā – he, who sits meaninglessly, uselessly, and in a tragic way, doing nothing, just as a lazy person. Such a person, in the language of the **Bhagavad Gita** and in the words of Bhagavan Sri Krishna, is a **mithyacarah** – a hypocrite, who shows he is a Yogi if he closes his eyes, does nothing with his hands and does not work or go out. He can pretend but he is only cheating himself because his mind is still attracted and tempted to worldly actions. So what should he do? First of all, he should either experience the world, or have control of his mind. If he cannot control his mind and cannot organize and control his senses it will finally be known that he is only pretending. There have always been people who pretend to be very pious. They like to pray in the street, at the crossroads, they go often to the temple, and people say how pious they are. Every Sunday people go to church; they say they are practising religion because they go to church every Sunday. We go to places of worship not to become pious but so that our hearts and minds become purified. People put on clean clothes to visit church, temple and mosque. That's nice, but the "inner clothes" should also be changed! They should not be full of anger, hatred, jealousy and evil thoughts towards others. All these things should not exist. Bhagavan Sri Krishna emphasized that a person pretending to pray or meditate, if he is not conducting a real meditation from inside, then his meditation is false behaviour. We should be careful of such a person.

Bhagavan criticizes such a person bitterly, and he shows the right path. The right way is not to control the body from outside but to control the personality, the individuality, from inside. Inner controlling, inner subduing, inner conquering, inner discipline is much more difficult than outer discipline. If we close ourselves in a room do you think that our mind will become pious? It will be wandering all around! It will be much better to go outside, than to close oneself in a room to meditate and say "I am meditating" in that case. We should not show off or disturb others when we meditate.

Peace of mind, silence of mind, quietude of mind, is a necessity for an individual. For this purpose you have come here. So, Bhagavan Sri Krishna says to Arjuna, "You are a responsible person and must behave in a responsible way. Your time to renounce the world has not yet come." Renunciation is not for all and sundry. It is only for a chosen few who have a developed mind, and evolved sufficiently inside. If spiritual evolution has not taken place, if the inner constitution is also unripe, then do you think the path of **Sannyasa** (renunciation) can be followed? They will fall, make mistakes because they have not yet fulfilled their span of evolution. Man has to evolve from inside. His constitution has to be developed.

Karmendriyāṇi saṁyamya – after having controlled the organs of action it is easy to sit down and meditate – but the mind is not meditating. When a beginner meditates he is thinking about the sense objects and that is why his mind is distracted and perplexed and disturbed. Everybody does not meditate easily. So as clean clothes are needed to put on our body, a clean mind is also needed for meditation. When you come for meditation you should know what are the preliminary necessities for meditation. Meditation is not that somebody can just come from outside and start to meditate. No, some preparatory work has got to be done. If we plough a field for planting we can't just throw the seeds anywhere. Stones, for example, will mar the growth of plants, so the stones must be taken out, along with the weeds. It has to be soft and nice soil for the seed to grow. In the same way meditation, too, and this can be done by the observance and practice of **Yama** and **Niyama**. According to Patanjali's **Sutras** these will lead us to Self-realisation. The concept is simple, the practice is difficult.**Yama** is comprised of five restraints or moral injunctions: **Ahimsa** (non-violence), **Satya** (truthfulness), *Asteya* (not stealing), **Brahmacharya** (celibacy), **Aparigraha** (non-possession). **Niyama** is comprised of five fixed observances: **Shaucha** (purity), **santosha** (contentment), **tapas** (self-discipline), **svadhyaya** (self-study), **iśvara pranidhana** (surrender to God).

You can see how deep the significance of this sloka is. It is full of potential. Merely by closing the eyes and ears, keeping the hands inactive, not using the legs and not working with the body, one cannot become a saint. **Karmendriyāṇi saṁyamya** – Bhagavan Sri Krishna asks Arjuna, "If you just control your organs of action, do you think that you are really a Yogi?" The approach of the **Bhagavad Gita** is subtle. Everyone is not called to meditate, there has to be a selection. Meditation is for some higher goal, higher achievement, higher spiritual experiences. That is why selection has to take place. So we call people, we sit together, we try to understand – but some people just go on their own way. That's the problem in ashrams. People stay for only a short time because their minds are occupied from outside with temptations and affections of life – which may seem apparently normal, but for meditation it is not.

For meditation there are conditions which have to be fulfilled. There are certain qualifications which are needed, and some of them we have briefly mentioned. Sometimes we ask people, "Why do you want to meditate? Do you want to, do you actually need it, and for what purpose?" Of course, meditation in most cases is useful and helpful – whatever we do, we will do it better and deeper than before. But it will not be so for a person who has apparently hidden himself from outward activities and is not ready on the mental plane. The task of meditation is to prepare the individual on the mental plane, and that is what Bhagavan Sri Krishna is doing – taking an inner approach. What an insight he has! He has scrutinized the mind of Arjuna. How great a psychologist he is! So, **Karmendriyāṇi saṁyamya** – on the controlling of our organs of action where it is not required in meditation. In meditation something more than the controlling of our organs of action is needed. People sit for meditation and they will be taught to control their organs of action, but if the mind is not controlled, not dominated, not disciplined, then the requirements of **yama** and **niyama** have not been met. Only by adhering to the principles of **yama** and **niyama** meditation is possible.

Even to sit for a short time is useful in our lives and perhaps we can attain the new layer of mind which Bhagavan Sri Krishna speaks about to Arjuna. **Manas! smaran** – Mentally such a hypocrite is running after the sense objects, his attraction is there towards the temptation of sensuous objects. How will he be able to meditate in the real sense of the term? It's not as if you should not enjoy the world, nothing to do with that. It is only for a person who wants to meditate that such a prescription is there. A prescription is needed in life sometimes and medicine is given. An ayurvedic physician will prescribe a medicine and tell you not to eat certain things, otherwise the medicine will not work. In the same way a prescription is given here also – if you want to meditate we will ask you not to do certain things. But then the medicine should be taken otherwise the mental difficulties will not be removed, and more will be created. That's what happens – people think they will simply just sit and meditate. No, first of all the diagnosis should be taken and the obstacles in the path of meditation seen. It is this that Bhagavan Sri Krishna mentions in this **sloka** – it is so beautiful, it is rational and comprehensible, and useful in our lives. Because we have such daily problems, we become restless, nervous, angry and lose our tempers, and criticise. All these things happen in every family, in every society. Some people speak about it, others do not, but then they suffer.

Bhagavan Sri Krishna is reminding his devotee Arjuna in this verse that one whose conduct is false, who pretends in the name of divine spiritual life, is not helping himself. Such pretension can bring admiration for a short time but it does not help us. How can it make our life healthy and prosperous? How are we brought alive? How are we in the divine state? How are we evolved from inside and in the divine life? How thought-provoking this one verse is! Bhagavan does not venture to say that you do not feel, that you do not see beautiful objects, nor hear beautiful sounds, as eyes and ears have been given us to see all this beautiful creation. He does not say, "do not see" but **see** the divine in all creation. And when you do that you are not hypnotised. Every human being becomes a living temple of God, a living image of God. So, if the world is seen from that point of view it becomes worth living. Bhagavan would say that this is the right way of seeing it.

Creation is joy – painters, singers, composers are all creators. Bhagavan Sri Krishna would not say don't do it; don't take part in beautiful music, **bhajans**, and **sankirtan** which uplift us. On the contrary he advises us to do so — such wonderful creation all around us to see, feel, hear, smell and understand. And it is not denied in this **sloka**, it is advised! Then what is denied? Attachment to sense objects. If attachment is not there you become just a pure witness. Detachment does not mean that your function, your activity is stopped, it means you will not be the slave of sensuous pleasures in the chains of bondage.

Verse 7

यस्त्विन्द्रियाणि मनसा नियम्यारभतेऽर्जुन ।
कर्मेन्द्रियैः कर्मयोगमसक्तः स विशिष्यते ॥ ७ ॥

Yas-tvindriyāṇi manasā niyamyā'rabhate'rjuna I
karmendriyaiḥ karmayogam-asaktaḥ sa viśiṣyate II 7 II

But he who controls the senses by the mind, o Arjuna, and without attachment engages the organs of action in the path of work, he is superior.

yaḥ – who so; tu – but, on the other hand; indriyāṇi – the senses, the sense organs; manasā – by the mind; niyamya – controlling; ārabhate – commences, engages in; Arjuna – O Arjuna; karmendriyaiḥ – by the organs of action; karmayogam – karma yoga, path of work; asaktaḥ – unattached; saḥ – he; viśiṣyate – excels.

Yas tu – tu is indeclinable in English. It means "his thinking is taking a turn", the thinking of Bhagavan Sri Krishna is taking a turn. In contrast to such a person (the hypocrite in verse 6), this is a different person - **yas-tvindriyāṇi manasā niyamya** – one whose organs are disciplined, unlike the former. **Niyamya** means properly disciplined, **manasā** means with the mind. People do not have discipline of their senses and organs. Here in this **sloka** Bhagavan Sri Krishna gives the inner attitude we should have towards life. The organs of action and the senses are disciplined not from outside, but with the help of the mind inside. The driver of a car doesn't control it from outside, he uses the brake and other controls from within the car. The driver, like the soul, is sitting inside. He himself is disciplined, so the car is disciplined, it is governed by the driver.

Similarly, you are like the driver of a chariot, for example. The chariot driver disciplines the horses properly, and if they are not, then there will be difficulties, and you will not be able to go to your destination, your goal. This body, as a chariot, and mind, as a driver, have been given to us in order to go to a goal, to attain divine life, to attain Yoga, to attain meditation in our life. This has been given to us purposefully – it is not meaningless. Without the horses the chariot will not move. If the horses are there but will not walk or run, you will be left standing and will not arrive at the destination. And if the horses are not properly disciplined, all will fall down into the ditch. What, then, is the right course?

The right course is that the driver is properly, equally, balanced in mind, perfect. Then the horses are properly disciplined with the help of the reins, so that they may carry the passenger, the one who sits inside the chariot, right up to the destination.

It is this that Bhagavan Sri Krishna is thinking of in this **sloka**. **Karmendriyaih karmayogam** – and then he performs the action, **Karma Yoga**. Action becomes the Yoga for him, meaning the source of union. Union with what? Union with the Self and communion with the Divine is Yoga. So, here the word **karmayoga** has been used. Action becomes **Karma Yoga** when we do not have expectation of the fruit of action. When actions are done in the Divine Consciousness, from the Divine point of view. Then, at that time, our life becomes divine.

It is this divine life which has been depicted in this verse, **asaktah sa viśiṣyate** – such a person is a distinguished person, a distinguished Yogi. It has been the purpose of Bhagavan Sri Krishna to tell us that action has got to be done. The body has to function, senses have got to be used. But in what way and how to use them? This art of living has been spoken of very deeply in this verse.

Verse 8

नियतं कुरु कर्म त्वं कर्म ज्यायो ह्यकर्मणः।
शरीरयात्रापि च ते न प्रसिद्ध्येदकर्मणः॥ ८॥

Niyataṁ kuru karma tvaṁ karma jyāyo hy-akarmaṇaḥ I
śarīrayātrā'pi ca te na prasiddhyed-akarmaṇaḥ II 8 II

Do thy allotted work, for action is better than inaction; even the maintenance of thy physical life (of the body) cannot be possible without action.

niyataṁ – bound, obligatory; kuru – perform; karma – action; tvam – thou; karma – action; jyāyah – superior; hi – for; akarmaṇaḥ – than inaction, inactiveness, non-performance of duties; śarīrayātrā – maintenance of the body (physical life); api – even; ca – and; te – thy; na – not; prasiddhyet – would be possible; akarmaṇaḥ – by inaction.

Bhagavan is again saying to Arjuna, "Look here, it is not proper to shirk your duty." This statement is very difficult and delicate. The world is so difficult that some people cannot adjust in society and sometimes they run and escape because it is too painful to face themselves. Even once in twenty-four hours people find it difficult to sit and do that! They will run about all over the place. We are not criticising their going around visiting the country – we have already spoken of this world as divine and beautiful. But how many people see it from this point of view? A few do, but otherwise people are just running, living a very hectic life. They are running about helplessly. They may be forced, obliged to do so, and sometimes they do it because they are restless and can't concentrate the mind – it would be a problem for them to sit. This sitting we do, even though for a short time, is the dawn of wisdom upon us. The Light of Knowledge begins to shine on us, and we sit, and begin to think a little.

And this is what Bhagavan Sri Krishna is trying to encourage His friend and devotee, Arjuna, to do. So, He is reflecting with Arjuna, saying, "**niyatam kuru karma tvam**" – deliver what you are supposed to and must do. Kuru is in the imperative mode so it is an ordinance, that you should do the duty which has been assigned to you, otherwise society will not be able to move, and even the body finally will not be able to move. Otherwise, why is everyone assigned to a duty, to an activity? To escape that duty is not right conduct. If we have an ethical way of life we will share in the social work of society. And if we do this work as Bhagavan Sri Krishna said in verse seven, "the one whose senses and organs of action are disciplined through the mind, his action becomes **Karma Yoga**", we come to feel that doing work for mankind is action for God and God alone. If such a beautiful attitude comes in society, how wonderful! Everyone will work in such a sensible spirit and work will become worship.

It is not the world, the outer form, that we have to change. Let the industries, the mills, universities and colleges remain where they are – the quiet transformation is in the hearts and minds of people, not in a block of stone, or in buildings or clothes. How much importance we sometimes give to walls, buildings and monuments – what about the monument of monuments which is a human being? More attention is being paid to the buildings, to the comforts of life and material needs. They are needed, they are indispensable, **but** see in them the Divinity. If such an attitude (work is worship) is inculcated in society, society will change overnight! You may say that that is utopia and cannot be realized but why not? We are filled with this kind of spirit and if right from today, or tomorrow, even if only a chosen few of us do so, what a great work will be done! For example, Buddha in the beginning was all alone and then five disciples took up the challenge of such a life as His and lived it. The most important thing is not the teaching, but living it moment to moment because teaching doesn't help unless we live it in our lives. That is why religion today has lost influence – people despise it because those who are teaching it are not living it. As soon as we begin to live the teaching, society changes. Vinoba Bhave, a disciple of Gandhiji's, used to say that great works are not done only by a material approach – great works are accomplished by soul-force.

What is this soul-force, this **ātma śhakti** – energy of the soul? As electricity pervades everywhere, even in the ether, in the same way the soul substance is everywhere. When you begin to work on the soul it means you are working everywhere, your message is going to all parts of the world just like a television station. Like the transistor radio, just tune it and immediately news and talk are received. They are in the ether. In the same way, much more subtle that the ether itself, is the soul, the **Atman** – the all pervading substance. When you become one with That you work for the whole world. In almost every country there are at least some people who know of Ramana Maharishi. This tiny person, sitting inside a cave, did so much magic in the world by giving the simple message: "Ask, 'who am I?'". Only this is sufficient he said. It is the Vedic teaching in a nutshell, pure non-duality.

Sri Shankarananda says in his commentary: The **Atman** (Self) is immobile, doesn't work, doesn't act. This has been realised by the great saints and sages. Where will it move, in which place is the **Atman** not? For example, we can move any object from one place to another because there is an empty place for it. But such is not the case with the **Atman** – there is no place which it does not fill, it is everywhere, it is all-pervading. If you identify your body with the **Atman** it is false – the body is not the **Atman**. Many people do take the body as the **Atman** and that is why from the beginning of their lives they are only working for the body. All work is done only for the body – food, clothes, shelter, luxuries, and inventions of all kinds. So, people have body consciousness. This is good in a way, but to identify it as the **Atman** and **Atman** alone, that is neither right nor proper because the body is not all-pervading. **Atman** is all-pervading, eternal. The body is not eternal; it is born, it grows, then after a time it decays, it disappears. But the **Atman** doesn't disappear at all. So the qualifications and attributes of the **Atman** do not hold good with this body as the body is not imperishable. The **Atman** is imperishable. Subject to death and decay, the body is changing from moment to moment.

So, this body changes and yet people have such a great attachment to it. If anything happens to it they will suffer because of this false identification with it. Most people think, 'I am the body, you are the body'. It is not that we should not look after it, feed, clothe, work it – that would be a wrong understanding. It has to be looked after because it is a manifestation of this omnipresent Reality. If this body would not be here then how would I realise this omnipresent Reality, that all-pervading Reality which is **Sat** (which means Existence)? That Self is Existence. **Atman** is Existence. This body is not. Today it exists but after one hundred years it will not exist. That is not the case with the **Atman**, which was existing in the past, exists at present, and will continue to exist in the future and after. Even when this body disappears the **Atman** will continue to exist because it is eternal in nature. So you can see that the qualifications, the attributes of the **Atman** do not hold good with the self (ego-self). Great souls considered the body as clothes. Just as a man discards clothes when they are old, in the same way the Self is just changing clothes – this body is the clothes on the Self!

Some people when they are frustrated, lazy, old or tired of life, don't want to do anything, not even look after the body. The body must be cared of and looked after for right up to the last moment. Cleanliness and purification of the body is very necessary and that is why we do **yajna** for purification of the body, heart, mind and atmosphere. **Yajna** is a Vedic activity – it has been prescribed by the **Vedas** and for us it is daily work. There is no place for laziness in Vedic culture. A politician once stated that Shankaracharya had completely ruined India because he taught inactivity! He totally misunderstood – inactivity (**naiṣkarmya**) is only for certain persons who have realised **Brahman**, those living in Divine Consciousness who have become one with everyone. But out of millions there is only one person like that! What the liberated one does or does not depends upon him – he cannot be forced to do anything, he is one with the Self. If ordinary people completely reject, deny activity, then even the body pilgrimage will not continue.

The teaching is there but one has to become aware of it, and it is for that reason we try to study the **Bhagavad Gita** and perform rites and ceremonies. For twenty-three hours a day we live in duality, in the world of plurality. Maybe for half an hour perhaps we meditate and reach an **advaitic** state. The message of Ramana Maharishi is not easy to realize and until we realize the **summum bonum** of life we have to work. The Vedic rites, ceremonies, chanting, singing, are not meaningless. These activities are meant for us until we reach the highest. Until then, we have to work.

This is actually what Bhagavan Sri Krishna is teaching in this verse. Being a highly elevated soul He understands the difficulties of people who are living on the lower planes of life. **Niyatam kuru karma tvam** – you have to work and do daily duties, you have to be responsible for that. **Karma jyāyo hy-akarmanah** – activity is superior to inactivity. Superiority of activity has been laid down in this beautiful verse – simple to understand but subtle in the whole system and fabrication of society. Society depends upon activity otherwise life would become impossible.

Śarīra means body, and just like a piece of cloth is torn out when it becomes old, so this body when it is old is also torn out. **Yātrā** means journey, and Sri Krishna is saying that the journey of the body will be impossible unless you mount it, drive it to its destination. Just by standing still at one place will not get you there! **Śarīrayātrāpi ca te na prasiddhyet** – even the journey of your life will not be accomplished in the least if you do not understand the importance of activity. Whilst driving this body like a chariot you must look after it, not neglect it. That's why we do **Yoga asanas** so that the body works for a hundred years and remains healthy – Yoga and meditation for a healthy mind. "A sound mind lives in a sound body."

If one is not liberated in heart and mind, liberation from outside will not do. The liberation of the soul depends only on the soul. It is all-pervading Reality and this is the kind of liberation everybody has the right to have. This is what we are trying to attain through these teachings of the **Bhagavad Gita** which is so sublime and noble that it makes us conscious of the all-pervading Reality. That is what actually you and I are. If I say this to you with mere words you will become aware for a moment, of course, but until you experience and realise it by yourself, you will not be convinced, and I will not be convinced. From the **Gita** teachings you will not be convinced, but it shows the means to Realisation.

Verse 9

यज्ञार्थात्कर्मणोऽन्यत्र लोकोऽयं कर्मबन्धनः ।
तदर्थं कर्म कौन्तेय मुक्तसङ्गः समाचर ॥ ९ ॥

Yajñārthāt-karmaṇo'nyatra loko'yaṁ karma-bandhanaḥ I
tad-arthaṁ karma kaunteya muktasaṅgaḥ samācara II 9 II

> *The world is bound by actions other than those performed for the sake of* Yajña *(Lord). Do therefore, o son of Kunti, earnestly perform action for* Yajña *alone, free from attachment.*

yajñārthāt – for the sake of sacrifice (Yajña); karmaṇaḥ – of action; anyatra – otherwise; lokaḥ – the world; ayaṁ – this; karma-bandhanaḥ – bound by action; tad artham – for that sake, for Him, for God; karma – action; kaunteya – o son of Kunti; mukta-saṅgaḥ – free from attachment; samācara – perform.

This **yajna** (fire sacrifice) that you have seen just now is a symbol. We kindled a fire and made an offering, pouring ghee (clarified butter), and **samagri** (herbs which come from the Himalayas) into the fire in order to purify the atmosphere. A simple thing that a child can do; a lay person can do. **Yajño vai viṣṇuḥ** (Taittiriya Samhita 1.7.4) – **yajna** is the form of **Vishnu**, God, who lives in everybody. **Vishnu** means God, who lives in everybody. It is not my God, nor your God. It is the God of the whole universe because He lives in everybody's heart, or rather, He has assumed the many forms of human beings, of all humankind.

We are using two commentaries for this **sloka**. One is the **Bhasyam** of Shankaracharya from the 8th century, and the other is the **Tika** of Sankarananda from the 15th century. **Bhasyam** is a verbal exposition, explanation, with discussion of a text; any doubts which arise in the minds of disciples and devotees are answered directly, at that time, by the master. Such commentaries were passed on orally down through the ages – many devotees knew them by heart. Now of course, we have this commentary on the **Bhagavad Gita** by Sri Shankaracharya in written form. A **tika** is a written commentary like the one authored by Sri Sankarananda.

The spiritual life is such that questions and doubts come into our minds. Out of hesitation we may not speak of them, and because of our lack of knowledge of spiritual or religious life (in the wider sense of the term), we suppress these questions. They then go into either our subconscious or unconscious mind and we suffer. Mental problems result. But if there is a person who can rightly give direction to our thoughts and ideas, and can help us resolve the doubts and problems, then we feel greatly relaxed; mental tension has been removed from our minds and we feel lightened and enlightened from inside.

In the past, great conferences called **sastrartha** were convened. Hundreds of scholars gathered together and discussed in details the pros and cons of the questions and doubts. There is not a question which was not answered by these great sages who are our ancestors. Today we may have forgotten such noble traditions, but the fact remains that when we go into them we are in such a different world. To do that, even while living in the thick and thin of our world today, is like drinking nectar! It is so pure – our mind becomes absolutely clean, thought is clear, systematic, and organized. All ignorance is dispelled, all darkness. We feel elevated. Life becomes methodical. That is why we dive deep into the **Bhasyam** of Shankaracarya. When we study at the holy feet of a sage the master goes slowly, explaining everything, showing us.

We can touch only briefly on **yajna**, the principle and concept of which comes to us from 10000 years ago, right from the Vedic culture. It is a great science, accurate and exact and is still being practised and studied here in India and abroad. In the word **yajna** the root is **yaj pujayam** – it means to worship.

Saints and sages were the worshippers of fire. Did they worship the flame? Is it the flame here, mixed with ghee and **samagri** that we worship? Fire has a deep and symbolic significance. Fire is latent in wood – wood is cold, when you touch it your hand is not burned, and it does not give heat energy. But when the wood is kindled, then the fire radiates and the whole atmosphere is surcharged with fire. This energy we need. We take it also from the sun, that is why we do **sūryopāsanā** – **sūryaḥ** means the sun and **upāsanā** means to sit close to, to worship. (**upa** – means near or close, **asana** – to sit). In worship we have to sit close to the fire or the altar. Energy is the same whether it comes from the sun, fire, electricity, oil, coal, ghee, or any other fuel.

The Mughal emperor Akbar cleverly heated water in the baths in his palaces by means of oil lamps. A lamp is a very small thing but it has so much heat and light. Flames and fragrances differ according to the oil which is burned, and each has a different effect on our consciousness. Oil is not destroyed in the flame but remains in the atmosphere and we breathe it in. The cycle of appearance and disappearance is continually taking place in nature and this is what the observers of **yajna** saw; anything which is burned no longer appears in front of us so we think perhaps that it is gone or reduced to ashes because we see the ash.

But no, it is transformed only – it has taken another form. These great **Rishis** may not have known chemistry or Dalton's laws or Newton's, or Einstein's theory, but they very well knew that nothing is destroyed in this world. Whatever was offered to fire they considered as God – they gave it a name, **Ishvara – Paramatma – Vishnu.** But what is this God? Fire? This fire is the only God which we worship; that apparent flame that is giving us heat has come out of the kindling of wood, a coarser form of the Divine. It is the Supreme Divinity, which is burning in the form of fire. We worship the Divine, and not the material fire.

The phenomenon itself is so mysterious. Fire is inside wood and wood may lie for months, years, and it will never give us heat. If it is analysed in the laboratory fire will not come, although in every atom and molecule there is latent fire. When a certain action is done, only then does fire come out of the wood, and it comes in flame which is so different from wood. Fire is as if condensed in the form of wood, of various oils, of ghee. As fire is in the wood, so is the Self in us. In meditation we kindle awareness of Self. The heat of the sun when focused through a lens can set things afire. Similarly, meditation is like the lens which enables us to concentrate the scattered rays of our mind. When the rays are concentrated the Self is enlightened. So, fire and energy are there, but all energies are different in their manifestations and experience, and have a different consequence on our consciousness. It has been well studied. Scientists in Europe are performing **yajna** and trying to analyse the scientific significance or effect on mind, thoughts, consciousness, and the medicinal effects also. It is a great field of research for psychologists, doctors of medicine and saints and scholars.

So, we are studying the deep and symbolic significance of this ninth **sloka**. Nothing is destroyed or wasted. We breathe – see what **yoga asana** you will perform if you will not have energy or strength in your body! The strength comes out of **yajna**. The great Yogis, saints and sages lived in the woods. The greatest culture of India grew in the forests. The third of the four **Asramas** is called **Vanaprastha** which means the **Asrama** of forest (**vana**). In this stage of life people left their village and city life and lived in an atmosphere of peace in the forest so that they could meditate, think, and contemplate the life that they have lived in the past. Vedic culture was beautifully classified, so decided, planned and organised. Afterwards it was disturbed and the disturbance continues. People are restless, isolated from the noble traditions which give beauty, strength and energy. Our way of being, of living is so deeply interwoven with this sacrificial fire ceremony.

Why do we consider that this fire is God? In the formless **nirakara** state it exists in the ether, in the atmosphere, but it is not visible. We give it a form in the sacrificial fire – to that which is formless we give form. How full of significance it is! And you begin to see the fire. An apple falls down in the orchard and even imbecilic goats and sheep see. Newton's eyes also saw and in that he found the law of gravitational force. It is the same thing in this fire ceremony. An ordinary person will only see fire, but an evolved person who is able to think about what this fire is will understand the esoteric significance which the Vedic saints and sages knew. And the fire ceremony provokes refined, purified, chaste thoughts in our mind, thoughts which are in everybody's mind, living there – latent. Mind is the same, it is the cosmic mind we are sharing. In you it is your mind, in me it is my mind, but then there is a collective mind, a collective consciousness, a universal mind, a universal consciousness which is called God, Brahman, **Ishvara**. You may give it any name. The Reality is One. **Ekam sad viprāḥ bahudhā vadanti** (Rigveda1.164.46), means the Truth is One, wise men call it differently.

Yajnārthāt-karmaṇon' nyatra loko'yam karmabandhanaḥ – Bhagavan Sri Krishna says, if you will perform actions apart from the yajna then this will be the cause of your bondage. Do you think that He means we should spend all twenty-four hours performing the yajna? We have to interpret these words in the modern context – that it is the spirit of offering our actions to God, not expecting any return or reward. In order to please God we perform the sacrificial fire, we do not expect anything but it comes back – all these offerings come back to us. How? The herbs, incense, ghee, go into the atmosphere, rain comes and brings them back to Mother Earth and thus come into existence the fields of grains and cereals. They go to purify the atmosphere, and purified come back, and so the cycle goes on, just as it was visualised by the great saints and sages of India.

And this ninth **sloka** can help us in the modern world, especially when India is trying to evolve materially; an industrial revolution is taking place. What is the place of this **sloka** in India today and in the world? It has a place because it is an attitude, it is a glimpse towards the life of which Sri Krishna speaks. **Yajnārthāt-karmaṇonyatra** – any action performed which is devoid of the spirit of **yajna**, of worship, will be the cause of our bondage. Simple truths, eternal truths have been spoken! It is not the ceremony only of which Sri Krishna and the saints and sages speak; that is only the symbol, the token of these Divine Principles. So, ordinary people who are working with the intention of getting a reward, the fruits of action, are bound, handcuffed.

They are bound **immediately** by the fruits of action – they do not see the fruit in the action itself.

As fruits live in the branches, and the branches and leaves are working for the fruit, the fruit comes – the tree doesn't eat! Just see! The **yajna** is taking place in the home of the tree. See how selfless the tree is, more so than we! The tree prepares its fruit but not for itself – **we** drink the nectar. In the same way, the river is flowing but she does not drink – we drink, animals drink, and the land is irrigated. What a selfless sacrifice is taking place. The river flows in nature as she is not bound. Let the river be bound by a dam and it will be stagnant, immediately polluted. So it is in our case if we cease to live the principle of sacrifice. It is in the Divine that this principle of **yajna** exists. That is why the sages said **yajno vai viṣṇuḥ** – **yajna** is God – in that sense as a principle, the principle of creation, of divinity. How significant this **sloka** is! It tells us to become devoid of attachments, to live in absolute freedom. **Mukta-sangaḥ samācara** – work in society but with the spirit, the attitude that your works are the offerings, the oblations to the Divinity. Then the action will not be the cause of bondage.

Read this verse and try to understand the deeper esoteric significance. Don't just memorise it. Don't cling to the words, go deeper and witness that Reality. Then life is filled with beauty, joy and happiness. This is not to become like a scholar, or to repeat the text like a parrot. Not that. Make an effort to understand it, and realise it and experience it in your life through devotional services.

Verse 10

सहयज्ञाः प्रजाः सृष्ट्वा पुरोवाच प्रजापतिः ।
अनेन प्रसविष्यध्वमेष वोऽस्त्विष्टकामधुक् ॥ १० ॥

Sahayajñāḥ prajāḥ sṛṣṭvā purovāca prajāpatiḥ I
anena prasaviṣyadhvam-eṣa vo'stv-iṣṭakāmadhuk II 10 II

*In ancient days the Lord of creatures (*Prajāpati*) created men along with sacrifice and said, 'By this shall ye increase and this shall be unto you that cow which will yield all your desires'.*

sahayajñāḥ – together with sacrifice; prajāḥ – mankind, the beings; sṛṣṭvā – having created; purā – in the beginning of creation, in the days of yore; uvāca – said; prajāpatiḥ – Prajāpati, the creator or Brahmā; anena – by this; prasaviṣyadhvam – shall ye propagate, shall ye multiply; eṣaḥ – this; vaḥ – your; astu – let be; iṣṭa-kāma-dhuk – the cow that yields all your desires.

Sahayajnāḥ prajāḥ sṛṣṭvā – saha means with, and **yajnah** means sacrifice. The fire ceremony connoted sacrifice of self, or ego, of self sacrifice. Ego is difficult to overcome – it is very painful to sacrifice ego. Ego causes many conflicts in relationships. When love is present ego does not exist. Love is God of all Gods, and it is such a God that it doesn't accept challenge from any side. It is the Supreme God, the God of love. The word **prajapatih** is used in this verse. **Praja** means creation and traditionally in India in the past, and at present, among noble families, creation (conception of a child) took place with great knowledge, wisdom and understanding, and with self-sacrifice. The sacrifice which takes place in the form of the fire ceremony is only the symbol of our inner sacrifice of our little ego – to abandon oneself for the sake of love of God. If we do not want to sacrifice our ego for somebody then at least we should know that creation will not be possible. And if creation is not possible then we shall be blocked somewhere because creation is the law of nature. And so long as we are on the natural plane, creation has got to take place, and it **cannot** without the sacrifice of the ego. Where there is sacrifice of the ego only then love is possible, creation is possible.

So, traditionally in India the act of creation does not take place haphazardly. You don't meet on the street and love! Or just live a very hectic life, move and run around without understanding the consequences. It was done with knowledge and understanding – that's why the word **yajnah** is used. **Yajnah** is not done without understanding, it is done with certain prayers and in these the invocation of the God of love is there. Just see it - before love there is an invocation to the God of love. If the God of love is not invoked (that means aroused) it doesn't come into existence; if creation takes place blindly, then the creature will also be blind in nature. He or she will do whatever he or she likes without thinking, without understanding.

You can understand that love is not a temptation. There is a great difference between lust, temptation and love. They are different things. That is why there can be love without temptation and lust. Lust is not something that is noble or acceptable or agreeable. And when something is not agreeable it has an irritable effect and anger, jealousy and hatred result. Lust breeds these three qualities, and yet it is the smoke of love before the fire burns! Lust, temptation, and seduction are the smoke of love. Lust is on the physical plane and can be said to be the gratification of the ego. Out of ego comes lust – "I just want to think of myself" –

and thoughtful consideration for the other is lacking. In love, I think of the other, give myself, sacrifice myself, for love is not possible unless I sacrifice myself. Love always requires sacrifice and sacrifice is painful, it is disagreeable. Giving is difficult, taking is easy. Even a child is grasping – he or she loves to take but seldom likes to give, and has the tendency to take, to receive, to accept. They do not know they have to give, and eventually, even to give their own selves. The most selfish person in this world has to give himself up completely. And until and unless this is done, love will not be possible, and creation will not take place. Eventually he has to give himself up; it is the law of nature.

You can see that the store of oil remains in the lamp until the flame is kindled. As soon as the wick is lit then the whole store of oil is given up spontaneously and naturally. Then the lamp does not keep the oil for its own sake, it doesn't want to possess. The possession is dispossessed. Why? Because there is a transformation – the transformation of oil into flame that sheds light. That is love. Love is like light, it is Self-enlightenment. **What** is that love in which Self-enlightenment has not taken place? That is why our love is imperfect and incomplete if Self-enlightenment has not taken place. Self-enlightenment is bound to take place if love is proper, normal, natural and spontaneous. That is why there is joy in giving. In giving we receive – the whole lamp receives the light, the whole lamp is enlightened! You do not need to see a lamp with another lamp. You can seek the lamp itself with the presence of flame in the light of the lamp. All objects around it are illuminated in the presence of the lamp, not only the lamp. So, the lamp illuminates the whole atmosphere, the whole space, and dispels darkness. See it please! Mark that it dispels darkness, or better to say that darkness is transformed into light. It is a process that is taking place. How wonderful to think about the first primitive person who discovered the simple lamp – that she or he took a vessel from the potter and then made a wick from cotton, and with oil kindled a lamp and out of it the flame came!

Once during the time of Deepavali (Festival of Illumination) when I was a small child, my mother asked me to kindle a lamp. The potter brought the lamps to our house, and then they were washed and my mother prepared the wick, and oil was poured into the lamps. When I kindled my lamp and saw the light coming out of the wick I felt that it was not coming from the wick but from my own self. It is such an experience for a child, which is why many children see this light for the first time with great surprise. And in fact it is a surprise – light which was latent in a wick becomes apparent and clear, visible, manifest, expressed. It is this which manifests in love, in devotion, in mutual understanding, in self-sacrifice. All that is needed is self-sacrifice. That's why the word **sahayajñāḥ** means 'with sacrifice'. **Prajāḥ** means creation. Creation is not like a potter taking a lump of clay and making a pot; creation does not take place like that. We create out of our own self, you don't need clay from outside. When you create a child you don't take a lump of flesh from outside. It is an invisible process taking place in every human being which is again the symbol of **yajna**. In **yajnah** there is a **vedi** in which you pour fire oblations. What is it? It is the same thing in which we consider the female principle to be like a **yajna vedi** herself, and a man is considered as performing the **yajnah** there. And it is in fact with this attitude that the **garbhadhan samskara** (the creation of a child) is carried out. The education of a child does not take place when she or he comes out of the heart (womb) of the mother. The real education takes place in the bosom of the mother. See, how the great soul and great Vedic seer Vamadeva came in to existence. He became self-enlightened in the womb of his mother and proclaimed, "I was the sun and everything in this universe". Why? Because his mother was meditating upon the Supreme Self while he was in her womb. That is the impression of the mother on her child. As the father is, so the child is; as the mother is, so the child is. The child is a consequence of the parents' love. It is love which incarnates, it is love which formulates, expresses, manifests. If the creation of a child is done with consciousness then a great soul will be born. That is why here in India the creation of a child is a **yajnah** and done with a great sense of prayer, of sanctification and with purity. People think of it as a sacrifice of self done at the altar.

Prajāpatiḥ is a nice term in itself – it is the God of love. God of love created, so creation was taking place in love. Real creation takes place in love, and the children of love are the children of great love. What did **prajapatih**, the Lord of creatures say? This sacrifice may become for you the means of satisfaction of all the desires you are seeking.

Traditionally in India only three of the four classes could participate in **yajnah**. These were the Brahmins (philosophers, wise men, saintly persons); the Kshatriyas (aristocratic warrior class); the Vaiśyas (people of commerce and business). What about the fourth class which are the Sudras? Who and what are they? Do they have to be despised, hated, not to be considered in the category of Brahmins, Kshatriyas or Vaisyas? Why was this fourth class kept? And why were they denied the rights given to the other three? The last-mentioned, for example, could participate in the fire ceremony but the Śudras were denied this right. In their case the purification ceremony has still got to take place and there are certain rules and regulations for self-purification. Not only body but mind and heart must become clean. We give so much importance to external cleanliness but if a man's mind, his heart, is not clean then total self-purification has not taken place. And in fact when the classes were selected it was according to their attributes and qualifications and their natural disposition of mind. So Untouchables should not be considered untouchable from the physical point of view. Gandhiji renamed them Harijan, meaning the people of God, and began a reforming movement for them. He said that in the next lifetime he would want to be born into a Harijan family. Justice has not been done to them.

It's quite all right to be a Brahmin, and they should be respected and worshipped because they have the knowledge of Brahman which means Divine Knowledge, sacred and ennobling. It cannot come to everyone and does not come to all. This cosmic consciousness is so easy to attain, but it is really very difficult for it is only when one dies and is reborn in life itself that this consciousness comes, not before. All the great saints said this. And we go through the same great torture inside and that's why we suffer in our life. Perhaps you do not know why you are suffering. You are suffering only because the preparatory process is taking place in you since you have come here. Here we are really working for the realisation of that cosmic consciousness which is Divine Knowledge. This movement, this revolution has to take place. One of the great persons who launched this movement was Sri Aurobindo.

What kind of movement did he launch? It was the movement of love, of devotion, of pure love for all mankind which he had realised in himself. You see, we talk but we don't realise, otherwise how is it that we fail to love in our private and public life? That love of which we speak cannot be showered upon one until a quiet mind is attained, until one has realised the quietude inside. For example, after attaining realisation, Aurobindo did not run after anybody because if he had done so it would not have been understood. It is more difficult to possess one's own Self first. Then shed the rays of love. See, when the sun rises it doesn't chase after anybody, it doesn't even knock on your door! The rays of the sun are waiting outside, just imagine! It is the person who opens the door and immediately the rays of the sun enter and the whole room is enlightened. The rays of the sun do not force themselves in – that is what I have learned in my life. In the early mornings I realised the beauty of the sun; the wind was also blowing, and I used to close the room against the wind because she forces herself in. The wind forces, and in love there is no force. Love is so spontaneous, like the rays of the sun it goes – but only when the chambers of love are open. When our nuptial chambers are open then at that time the ray of love in our heart enters. It doesn't make any effort, it is the most effortless process. And that is only possible when a person has become ready for that! If one is not ready then how to receive it? That is why one has to have infinite patience and, if we do not have it then we cannot face things, we escape.

Prajapatih, the God of love created the world and that creation has taken place out of self-sacrifice. That is why the word **sahayajnah** is used. Now these are the things which are difficult to explain in the translation! In the commentaries and sub-commentaries things have been explained deeply – the translations cannot do justice to the Sanskrit. In lust we grab, but in love we share and give, just as we are giving here. What we give is not given anywhere as you give by your presence, your thoughts and ideas. There was sharing on the material physical plane. Now we are sharing on the spiritual plane, and if this sharing – for which we are staying here – does not take place, then all the sharing remains inadequate and incomplete. In every family there is a problem. Why? Because the sharing is not integral, it is not a sharing of the whole. Love is whole, integral, a Gestalt conception of love. Love is self-sacrifice and so ego must be sacrificed.

Verse 11

देवान् भावयतानेन ते देवा भावयन्तु वः ।
परस्परं भावयन्तः श्रेयः परमवाप्स्यथ ॥ ११ ॥

Devān bhāvayatānena te devā bhāvayantu vaḥ I
parasparaṁ bhāvayantaḥ śreyaḥ param-avāpsyatha II 11 II

You nourish the gods with this. Let those gods nourish you. Nourishing one another, you shall attain the supreme good.

devān – the gods, Indra and others; bhāvayata – nourish, cherish; anena – with this (sacrifice); te – those; devāḥ – gods, Devās; bhāvayantu – may nourish, may cherish; vaḥ – you; parasparam – one another; bhāvayantaḥ – nourishing, cherishing; śreyaḥ – good; param – the highest; avāpsyatha – shall attain, shall gain.

Devān bhāvayatānena – the god*s (***devas***)* shine forth, they radiate light, they are the source of enlightenment, of divinity, divine nature. This light is in all of us, and some people are aware, others are not. Just as it is the same light in all the stars and cosmic bodies, irrespective of their size, so it is the same light in us however small or great we are. And when we sit here and talk to each other, a kind of integration of that light in us is taking place because **you** are aware of it. In contact with each other, together, we are discovering that light which is already in you. You do not get this light from outside. The lamp burns with oil and a wick. It is not that the light has started from the match-stick. If it has come only from the match-stick, and water instead of oil was used, then light is not transferred in the same way, the light is not in the same proportion. But with oil the light is there, so when the wick is kept in oil and kindled, light becomes apparent, visible, and comes out in the form of a flame. The light enlightens the lamp and the objects around. Darkness is transformed into light. So, when you are restless and do not have peace of mind, you are running about trying to go many places, you are extroverted – light is absent outside. But when you become introverted, when you have come into contact with yourself, and in Yoga, and in meditation and during this time of **satsang**, we become aware, conscious, Pure Self-awareness grows in us and that makes us peaceful. That Self is in all but only the awareness is lost. So we become aware about the Self that dwells in all when we meditate. We are human beings and we go very often by trial and error methods, so we are likely to commit mistakes.

Sitting here we swim in the current of knowledge and thinking in the heart and mind of each other and thereby start a kind of fermentation, a kind of fusion, of integration, and this is very important. The awakening of great souls casts such a great influence on the mass of people, on the greater part of society. What does it mean when I say awakening – after all, aren't we all awake in the daytime at least? It is an awakening – from the worldly point of view – where you are awakened to the exterior, objective world, the world of duality, of plurality. This awakening is also needed for our practical application. And then there is another awakening to which Buddha came and thereafter was called **Bodhisatva**. The root **budh** means to be awake. So **Bodhisatva** means to be awakened to the **Sat** (Existence), to that which exists. Because that unity **only** exists, all that we are seeing is an appearance of it. There is existence and then there is an appearance. Usually people are awakened to the appearances but seldom are they awakened to the existential reality – the Reality of Existence on which this appearance is being projected. We are appearing to each other because we are projecting, but we are projecting on something that is real, because this which we are seeing, is also changing very fast from moment to moment like a flame.

A flame is changing incessantly. It is travelling, moving, changing very fast, but then it is shedding a light which is an integrated whole – something real in the form of light which enables us to see. When I was a student of physics my professor said to me, "Light is that which enables us to see; we don't see the light", and I was disillusioned because I always used to say, "I see the light"! It is interesting that we don't see light because our eyes cannot see its frequency. It is so small, so subtle that our eyes cannot detect it, but this light enables us to see. It is almost the same thing – we do not see the Existential Reality with these eyes because the Reality enables us to see what we are seeing all around. This Existential Reality is All in All, a continuous whole subject, on which all projection takes place.

In the waking state of consciousness there is the material world, and the material objects you are seeing, the world, is outside – something out of you which you can touch, see, smell, taste. So, in this world of the waking state of consciousness we are living in the world of duality. The same person who is in the waking state of consciousness and seeing this objective reality, is the same Self who also goes in the dream state of consciousness. You create it out of your own Self, this world of the dream. For that, you do not need brick and mortar from outside, all is created out of your own Self, completely. You do not depend on anything from outside. For example, when you are assembling this lighted lamp you have to depend on outside things, you have to go to the market and buy oil and wick. But in the dream state of consciousness nothing is done like this. You have completely yourself, and out of Self a world of duality is created which is – in a sense, and you know it very well – different from the waking state of consciousness in the sense that as soon as you are wakened it disappears. And you are wakened eventually! Your dream will last for eight hours, it does not last eternally, and then you are wakened and as soon as you are wakened then this dream is broken and there is no residue. There is nothing that is left after a dream. It is like a firebrand moved fast in a circular motion. If it is moved quite fast it appears to be a circle of fire. Is a circle created, does it really exist? If you say it exists then it should continue to exist, but it does not. As soon as you stop the movement you do not see the circle of fire any more. It is an appearance. In the same way out of yourself you create a dream. The circle of fire came out of the point of the firebrand, it also disappears into that when the movement stops. It is no longer visible, but there is some kind of illusion to our eyes. You make a circle and it appears. You cannot say it is completely false, but it does not completely exist. If it had been completely unreal, then you would not have seen it at all, or you would have seen it even when the firebrand was motionless. By moving the firebrand fast a circle is created. In the same way there is something – energy – left, or it is there, which expresses itself inside the dream. That energy creates, a creation takes place in the Self and out of the Self you create a world of which you are the monarch, the king, the master. It came out of you and this dream state of consciousness comes to all and sundry. To the wise and unwise, to women and men, to small children and to grown-up children.

This dream is such a phenomenon that it is witnessed by everybody. Vedantic thinkers and seers spoke about this dream state of consciousness as a state of consciousness of the Self in which everybody begins to see the dream as reality. And you cannot doubt the existence of the dream because you see it. Actually if it is horrible you can be frightened. If there is a lion inside the dream, you start to scream. So you cannot say that it is unreal, that it does not exist, that it is not there. But you cannot say also that it is real, because had it been real, then it would have lasted after you were awake, but it doesn't happen in reality. Something which lasts forever exists in the three tenses – past, present, and future. But such is not the case with the dream – it was not in the past and it does not remain in the future, it remains in the time being where you have created it. So it is with this touchstone that we come to realize that it is something ephemeral, because it lasts for a short time. So it is not real in the absolute sense of the term. It has a relative reality – you cannot say that that is completely unreal because had it been unreal then you would not have seen it for let us say eight hours. It is the same about this waking state of consciousness which lasts for 80 or 100 years. And after that time when the departure from this world takes place, you do not see it any more. Please try to understand and visualize this; it is very important because it is a crucial point in **Advaita Vedanta**. You see human beings, you see beauty everywhere, go to different countries. You meet people, talk to them, eat with them. They invite you, they are your friends, you like and love them, they like and love you. You like it so much that you are tempted to go there again and again – you cannot see that it is unreal.

You cannot say that there are horns on a hare's head, because horns do not exist on a hare's head. They absolutely do not exist, so you cannot see them. You can't see flowers in the sky – they do not grow there, they grow on the Earth. Horns grow on the cow's head so it is an absolute unreality to see horns on a hare's head because they do not exist. Flowers don't grow in the sky, they need the earth. The flowers that you continue to see on earth are real. You cannot deny them and you should continue to see them until they fade, and again in a new year the flowers will come. Fruits will come. You satisfy your hunger, you feed yourself – and in fact they feed you. In the same way you love human beings. It will last for some time. After a while, you do not see them, then you will sulk, be sad, because you want to cling. You want that feeling to be eternally in you – you want to realise that love as an eternity.

The desire for realising the eternal love is there in you. It is already evident that there is something eternal which we are not realising in this world outside. Bhagavan Sri Krishna has said in the second chapter, verse 28, **avyaktadini bhutani** – which means all beings come from the unmanifest state of consciousness. Before birth, for example, where were you? – before conception? You were not experiencing anything because you were in the unmanifest state. You were there, you were not absent. You have not come from nothing, you have not come from a vacuum, from the void (**sunyata**) where there is nothing absolutely – nothingness. There was something out of which you were coming but that was in the state of non-manifestation. The manifestation was not there, the clarity was not there and therefore you were not experiencing the world. A newborn baby opens his eyes and looks in all directions. It is surprising how he is discovering the world because only a moment before he was in a dark chamber, enclosed in a small balloon where there was perhaps not so much light, except liquid. He was enclosed in the heart of the mother; the light was not effulgent, not complete. He opens his eyes in an unconscious effort to see the world. That means he wants to discover it. And this discovery is in fact a creation of the world for him. What we are discovering we are creating, consciously or unconsciously. The Advaitic Vedanta thinkers were conscious that in unveiling and discovering the world there was a creation, just as with the sun it appears that it is creating the world outside. In the darkness the world was there but was not visible. So in a particular sense of the term, the creation has taken place with the rays of the sun, because it becomes visible to you!

Inside the dream there is also a creation; you cannot say that it is non-creation completely. Had it been a non-creation then you would not have seen it. You cannot see the dream in the waking state of consciousness because it is not there, you have not created it. You are seeing the waking state of consciousness, all right, but you do not see the dream state of consciousness during the waking state of consciousness. You are creating it. This time and space is a relative conception, even inside the dream vis-à-vis the waking state of consciousness. Similarly, the dream is a relative conception, and after some time you dissolve it, and the dissolution takes place in you, in your own Self. The dream came out of you, you projected it – the projection took place outside the Self, it is nothing different from your own Self, and again you absorbed it like a spider in to your own Self. The spider, for example, projects thread and creates such a magnificent cobweb outside. So there is a duality. The Upanishads, in order to explain the non-dual state of consciousness of this world, often give the example of the spider. Like a spider, a human being is projecting this world outside, he is creating the world out of himself, out of the Self. I think, I have an idea, and then execute this idea with my will, my energy, and this energy just transforms itself and creates what I see – humans, trees, mountains, rivers and all things – a relative reality which exists outside.

At the time of departure from this world it is as if the dream has come to a state of standing still, as if it is broken. It must be a surprising phenomenon. In some cases it is very peaceful, and for those who have seen a dreadful life the departure is a dreadful thing. It is not a horrible process – it depends upon the individual as to how she or he has led their life. Saints and sages trained themselves in such a way that when the time came for their departure they did so consciously, at a time and place of their choosing. Each of us is in a finite body and it is true that it helps us to realise the Infinite. There is no doubt that it is a very important instrument. When I am talking with you I become aware of this Infinite Reality, so I am realising that Infinite Reality. But with what? With the mental instrument – with the body.

Our body must be strong enough because it is a very important means of Self-realisation. In Yoga we realise our Self – it is meant for this, so you should know why we do Yoga, and meditate, and do **asanas**. Self-realisation is the **summum bonum** of life which has been described in the fourth line of this eleventh verse, – **śreyaḥ param-avāpsyatha.** Param śreyah means the **summum bonum**, the supreme good, the emancipation, the liberation. So this body, however fragile it may be, or limited, gives me the possibility of having glimpses of, and tasting, the Reality which is infinite, all-pervading, omnipresent. Discovery is the joy of Self-realisation, so please always think of it and do not confine yourself to this body. It is very important that you do not discover the Self only in this body because you are not only confined to this body. When we think that "I only" live in this body and identify with it, then that is a wrong identification. We cannot limit Eternity. Your real Self lives in me also, and my real Self lives also in you.

We are limited because certain kinds of conditions of the mind are there, and it may be good for our nourishment, because a fence is needed when we are a small plant so that we may not be hurt, nor eaten up by somebody! Such conditions come from religions, traditions, languages, or from nations. They help us to grow and are beautiful, but we must de-condition ourselves as we grow. We have to transcend this conditioning to realise the joy of Transcendental Reality. We must burst out of the cocoon of conditioning like a caterpillar. If the caterpillar does not burst its cocoon then it will die. And that is what is happening to the people outside in the world, because they do not outgrow it, they do not transcend the cocoon which they have created. The cocoon is a help to growth when you are immature, unripe, but when you are ripened it can also be an impediment, an obstacle, and mar our growth. The space inside the cocoon is so small! See, sometimes many people die when they do not burst out of it, just as many little caterpillars die inside the cocoon. If a baby inside the womb, a safe and secure place where everything is provided, wants to remain there, what will happen? It will be dangerous for mother and child. In Divine Creation it is not allowed, it is not done, however painful the process is.

See the growth that is taking place in you, take account of it when we sit in meditation. See that in the waking state and dream state of consciousness there is only the One Self.

Verse 12

इष्टान्भोगान्हि वो देवा दास्यन्ते यज्ञभाविताः ।
तैर्दत्तानप्रदायैभ्यो यो भुङ्क्ते स्तेन एव सः ॥ १२ ॥

Iṣṭān-bhogān-hi vo devā dāsyante yajñabhāvitāḥ I
tair-dattān-apradāyaibhyo yo bhuṅkte stena eva saḥ II 12 II

Being nourished by sacrifices (yajna), the Devas (gods) shall bestow on you the enjoyments you desire. A thief is verily he who enjoys what is given by them without returning them anything.

iṣṭān – desired for; bhogān – objects; hi – so; vaḥ – to you; devāḥ – the gods, the devas; dāsyante – will give, distribute; yajñabhāvitāḥ – being cherished, nourished, satisfied by yajña (sacrifice); taiḥ – by them; dattān – given; apradāya – without offering; ebhyaḥ – to them; yaḥ – who; bhuṅkte – enjoys, gratifies only his own body and organs; stenaḥ – thief, stealer of the wealth of gods and others; eva – verily; saḥ – he.

In this material world a lot of facilities and amenities have been given to us which are the result of the sacrifices of several people. For example, the newborn baby is nursed and brought up, which is a sacrifice by the parents. When the young are being educated, that is the sacrifice of the builders of the educational institutions. The food we are eating, the clothes we are wearing, all this is due to sacrifices made by other people who worked for it. Also, we should not forget that all the necessities of life, like grains, fruits, vegetables, etc. are supplied by the Lord. He produces sunlight, moonlight, rainfall, etc., without which no one can live. So our life is dependent on supplies from God, from others, with the purpose that we should make proper use of them to keep ourselves healthy for the purpose of Self-realisation, leading us to the ultimate goal of life, which liberates us from the material struggle for existence. This aim is attained by performance of **yajna** (sacrifice). If we forget this purpose and we just take the supplies which are given by the Lord, by others, for sense gratification and we entangle ourselves more and more in the material existence, we really become thieves. Such a person is called, according to the **Gita**, a thief. A thief is someone who grabs everything and sacrifices nothing, who enjoys or pleases his body and sense organs and who, not thinking of others, performs actions with a selfish motive in order to gain name, fame, honour and praise. Such a person shall be punished by the law of nature. He will never gain purity and peace of mind. A righteous person would never behave like this. He would, all the time in each task in life, first ask himself how his life is beneficial for others; what will be more useful for others. He will give more than he has received.

Verse 13

यज्ञशिष्टाशिनः सन्तो मुच्यन्ते सर्वकिल्बिषैः ।
भुञ्जते ते त्वघं पापा ये पचन्त्यात्मकारणात् ॥ १३ ॥

Yajñāśiṣṭāśinaḥ santo mucyante sarvakilbiṣaiḥ I
bhuñjate te tv-agham pāpā ye pacanty-ātmakāraṇāt II 13 II

> *The good people who eat what is left from the sacrifice are released from all sins but those wicked people who prepare food for their own sake – verily they eat sin.*

yajñaśiṣṭāśinaḥ – who eat the remnants of Yajña (sacrifice); santaḥ – the righteous, the good; mucyante – are freed; sarva-kilbiṣaiḥ – from all sins; bhuñjate – eat, incur; te – those; tu – but; agham – sin; pāpāḥ – sinful ones, unholy persons who are selfish; ye – who; pacanti – cook; ātmakāraṇāt – for their own sake, for themselves.

Yajnaśiṣṭāśinaḥ means that which is left after offering to the Divine. We offer to the Divine and then whatever is left we take. It only means that we are conscious about the Divine. After all, the Divine does not eat – even if you offer – as we eat, so everything remains there. It is we who eat. Here we offer food to the deity of Bhagavan Sri Krishna because we have that kind of faith. **Yajna** means to worship, and that which is left **Yajnaśiṣṭāśinaḥ** (partakers of the remnants of sacrifices), is a person who has such a nature that habitually he takes food after offering it to the Divine so as to have Divine consciousness even while eating. You see, animals also eat, and eat with great gusto. But I don't know actually if they have the Divine Consciousness – they feel hungry and in order to satisfy the hunger they eat. They also justify themselves, that because they are hungry they should eat. We are superior to them, and we become aware, conscious, about the Divine Principle that exists in the entire universe and which is in all of us, everybody. So, while taking food we are grateful to the Divine. Our attitude is one of gratitude, and we should be grateful to Him who feeds us.

And also be grateful to those whom we feed. Why? Because in India we think that a guest who comes to our family without being known is considered a **deva**, a god who comes in the form of a human being. We still have this kind of tradition in the villages. In the cities it is disappearing but in the villages people are very simple. So if a person arrives in a village all of a sudden the villagers treat him very nicely because of this belief. Because God comes unknown – **when** He comes we do not know. This tradition of hospitality still exists but not in big cities where people do not have the time – they are busy with their own private and personal lives with no time to think of others. When cities become big there are many facilities but there are disadvantages also and people become very much isolated – they don't know their neighbours, their friends and brethren. They live very much in themselves and every individual becomes an independent entity, living usually for his own self. This should not be the case. In fact, city life should bring us together, it should have some kind of consciousness that lives like a thread in all of us. And that is what we try to nourish, at least mentally here, and we become conscious of that Divine Principle that exists in all of us.

At the time of eating food, if there is Divine Consciousness then the food becomes divine. That is why we have the custom before taking food of chanting a small prayer. I think this tradition exists in all kinds of faiths, of thanking God – Father, Mother – who has given food.

So, this is what **Yajnaśiṣṭāśinaḥ** means – those who take the food after offering to the Divine; **mucyante sarvakilbiṣaiḥ** – they are liberated from all evils in this life; **bhunjate te tv-agham pāpā ye pacanty-ātmakāraṇāt** – on the contrary, those people who only eat for their own sake have no consideration for the Divine. They say, "Where is He, what is He, where does He live, what does He do? *We* do it, *we* prepare it, *we* work for it, so *we* eat. And not only that, we do not want to think of the Divine!" They also do not think of their fellow beings, they just eat for themselves, nourishing their bodies and are satisfied. Such people are called egoistic and there are many such people in every society – we do not know what we can say about such people! But somehow or other Bhagavan doesn't seem to appreciate them very much. After all they exist, they are a part and parcel of society. So it appears to me that he is criticising that portion of society that just feeds itself, and only looks after its own self.

I am reminded of Vinoba Bhave who years ago launched an all-India movement for land for landless people. The movement was called **Bhudana yajna** – **bhu** means earth, **dana** means donation and **yajna** means offering. In requesting the landlords, princes, kings (those who were big holders of land) to donate land to the poor who were landless, Vinoba Bhave said: "As sky, air, light, water, belongs to all, so also does this Mother Earth." That was a wonderful commonsense observation which we all liked, and once upon a time in India this movement was widely appreciated and land was donated. It began on 18th April 1951 in the village of Pocampalli in the district of Telangana in Andhra Pradesh where people had killed each other for a bit of land. As a disciple of Gandhiji, Vinoba Bhave was deeply touched and moved by this incident and he wept when he addressed the people of that district. He told them, "I cannot understand how it is that people can kill for a piece of land which is like our Mother, which belongs to all of us. So we should be courteous and generous and we should think that this land does not belong to a particular person, just as the sky, the light that comes from the sun, the wind, air and water flowing from rivers belongs to everybody. In the same way the earth belongs to everybody." If you think about it you will also see it as commonsense. Right from here you can go to any part of the world. It is a continuous whole globe – you can go anywhere, to any country, to any continent. Go wherever you like, this land is a continuous whole. But we have divided it. For the sake of practical purposes it is classified and organised but it is when the sense of possession comes that there is difficulty.

And this difficulty came to the mind of Vinoba Bhave, a great saint of our time. I had the opportunity to sit at his feet, and to walk with him on his **Padayatra** (pilgrimage on foot) for the landless. So I saw how he requested the landowners to think of the poor people who were landless: "In order to till they need land, and if you give them land they can cultivate it and can look after themselves." So it was purely an ethical, moral and spiritual outlook and India is a wonderful country from that point of view – that in the name of real Divine Life, if one has sincerity and honesty of purpose, then one has great grace in the hearts of people here. Why? Because such a person becomes one with the poorest of the poor. That was Gandhiji, in fact. That was the tradition of all the great saints in India that they became one with all. For them there is no sense of distinction, no racial, caste or religious discrimination. Such a person is a

Self-realised, Divine-realised, God-realised person. Naturally, people observe him and see that his attitude to all is equal and such a person casts a great influence. In the beginning it was only a piece of land that was given, then afterwards it was whole villages, and a time came when even cities were donated in India.

The Prime Minister at that time was Pandit Nehru and he came to sit at Vinobaji's feet. Both of them were sincere and honest disciples of Gandhiji. One of them, Vinobaji, was walking spiritually in India, from door to door, village to village. His movement was launched in the villages with the same thinking and in the same spirit as Gandhiji had. Villagers may be illiterate but they have great commonsense and wisdom and they immediately seized the significance of a great soul. Spiritual movements do not succeed so much in the big cities, they should begin in the villages – that was Gandhiji's experience.

There were always about twenty-six people accompanying Vinobaji and we averaged about 16 kilometres a day. In each village we worked very hard with the villagers. At the end of the day we would be very hungry. The food we were given was boiled vegetables in which there was no salt at all – it could be added if wanted when served. Whatever the vegetables and grains grown in the village fields were what was given to us. The taste that came in the village food after the hard labour on the land for these poor people was such a joy! And if we have good health today it is because of that work we did when we were young. Work, which was for ourselves, because they are not different from us – while working for the poor you are working for your own Self! A real saint, a Yogi, is one who has established identification with the poorest of the poor and the richest of the rich. God lives in both.

In the beginning Gandhiji was all alone and he used to say, "When you are alone working for the people don't think that you are alone. God is with you." Vinoba Bhave said the same thing, and also, "The sun is alone and it shines in the whole world." So with this spirit we do not think about numbers, we think of the quality of the work.

Vinobaji was a great teacher of the **Bhagavad Gita**. He used to teach anyone who came to him in order to learn Sanskrit **only** through the **Bhagavad Gita**. It is out of this book that Gandhiji and Vinobaji launched their movements to solve the problems of society, even social problems. They have solved even the economic problems of India with the help of the **Bhagavad Gita** because spiritual life is the backbone, the heart's blood of India, it is inseparable. Those who worked with Vinobaji have witnessed how the landless became landowners. They till the land and whatever they contribute they get the reward of it. So this is called **Bhudan Yajna**.

In this thirteenth verse and the preceding ones the word **yajna** is used. This word **yajna**, which is a Vedic fire ceremony, has to be given a wider interpretation, which is what Gandhiji, Vinobaji and other saints, and all who worked for social emancipation, have given it. So even the donation of land was called **yajna** because the land which we offer to God belongs to everybody. The land was offered in worship and adoration. So people in India worshipped their God with Mother Earth, they offered it to Him because She belongs to Him. A simple Indian proverb says: 'All land belongs to Gopal (name of Krishna, God) and there is no obstacle in this land anywhere. Only a person who has an obstacle in his mind has the obstacle outside, all over the land; otherwise there is no obstacle.'

Gandhiji asked that the youngest child in each family be given a handful of grain to place in a pitcher, and when it was full it was distributed to poor people. In this way the child developed the **Samskara** (habit) of thinking of and giving to others. The child feels joyous to give to anyone who comes, even to a bird, or dog or cat. The joy is the joy of our own Self because in all these things it is the same Self. In fact, every form is the incarnation of the same Self – the thing is, we sometimes forget it. That was the basis for Gandhiji's and Vinobaji's actions. Feeding the poor people and eating afterwards is also **yajñaśiṣṭāśinaḥ**. It is God in the form of poor people and so it is **yajna**, **puja**, to feed them, and it is a great joy. We do not eat only for the sake of ourselves, we do not nourish only *our* body, and we should try to think of this verse when we eat. When we start living with this spirit then we understand the teachings of the **Bhagavad Gita**.

Verse 14

अन्नाद्भवन्ति भूतानि पर्जन्यादन्नसम्भवः ।
यज्ञाद्भवति पर्जन्यो यज्ञः कर्मसमुद्भवः ॥ १४ ॥

Annād-bhavanti bhūtāni parjanyād-annasambhavaḥ I
yajñād-bhavati parjanyo yajnaḥ karmasamudbhavaḥ II 14 II

From food creatures come into being, from rain food is produced, from sacrifice arises rain and sacrifice is born of action.

annāt – from food; bhavanti – come forth, are born; bhūtāni – beings, creatures; parjanyāt – from rainfall; annasambhavaḥ – production of food, origin of food; yajñāt – from sacrifice, from yajña; bhavati – arises, originates; parjanyaḥ – rain; yajñāḥ – sacrifice; karmasamudbhavaḥ – born of action , born of karma.

Generally the word **yajna** stands for offering of oblation to the sacred fire. But here **yajna** denotes the performances of all duties, life oblation, charity and penance. In oblation food and purified butter, in penance pleasure, in charity selfishness and comfort are renounced. So all the actions performed without selfish motive as laid down in the scriptures are included in the term **yajna**. So it has to be understood that this **sloka** does not speak of the sacrificial actions themselves, but about the subtle principle into which they are converted, after having been performed.

Anna means food which is eaten in order to nourish the body. From the food all creatures such as men, birds, beasts, trees, plants are born and nourished with it. It is a matter of direct perception that – **annat**, from food – what is eaten is transformed into blood and semen and all the articles of food are produced from rain. The **smritis** say: "The oblation properly poured into the fire reaches the sun, from the sun comes rain, from rain comes food and from that the creatures." How will it rain through the sacrifice, through **yajna**? In verse 11 it has been said that if men perform their duty, the gods will also perform their duty by nourishing men through rain. Understand the work performed with the right attitude of mind gets converted into **yajna**. The effect of that work assumes a subtle force which is called in Vedic terms **apurva**. Just as the sun converts the sea water into the invisible vapour, in its turn the vapour becomes rain. This is the celestial **yajna**. Similarly, man's **yajna** changes into mental force which is **apurva**. It is the thought or the feeling and not the words while chanting the mantras that really constitutes the mental force. The purer the man and his motive, the stronger is the mental force. It is the intensity of the force of mind that becomes **apurva**. Influenced and regulated by it, the rain falls on the earth and naturally the production of grains, vegetables, etc. depends on the availability of water caused by rain.

Verse 15

कर्म ब्रह्मोद्भवं विद्धि ब्रह्माक्षरसमुद्भवम् ।
तस्मात्सर्वगतं ब्रह्म नित्यं यज्ञे प्रतिष्ठितम् ॥ १५ ॥

Karma brahmodbhavaṁ viddhi brahmākṣarasamudbhavam I
tasmāt-sarvagatam brahma nityaṁ yajñe pratiṣṭhitam II 15 II

Know that karma (action) has its origin in Brahma *(the* Veda*) and* Brahma *springs from the Imperishable. Therefore the all-pervading* Brahma *ever rests in* yajña *(sacrifice).*

karma – action; brahmodbhavaṁ – arisen from Brahman, arisen from the Vedas; viddhi – know; brahma – Veda, Immutable; the supreme Self. (Since the Veda came out, like the breath of a man, from the supreme Self, It is called the immutable. The Veda is the revealer of everything. He is all-pervading and imperishable); akṣara-samudbhavam – arisen from the imperishable; tasmāt – therefore; sarvagatam – all-pervading; brahma – the Veda; nityaṁ – always; yajñe – in sacrifice; pratiṣṭhitam – is established.

Karma brahmodbhavam viddhi – *karma* means action (you can call this work), activity; **bramodbhavam viddhi** means are born out of the Supreme Reality which has come in the form of the **Vedas.** So here the word **Brahma** has been interpreted as **Veda** and **Veda** means the storehouse of knowledge, abode of knowledge, source of knowledge, wisdom and cognizance. The root word is *vid* which means to know, and **Veda** is a noun out of the same root. So, **Vedas** are the abode of knowledge – they are not only the books which were written afterwards. Knowledge is in fact formless. We have invented letters, words, sentences, and the books came into existence. But in the context of this verse it does not mean the form – it means formless. The action we see – the movements of our limbs and the activity we are all performing – is only the outer manifestation of the inner activity that is taking place in all of us. The activity, in the form of energy, is in all of us stored in the latent potential form. It assumes the kinetic form and the various parts of our bodies move.

It is because of this energy that we are set in motion, that we are working. If we are devoid of energy we say we are tired which means we have exhausted the energy which was there and cannot even move to get ourselves a glass of water. Sometimes in this modern civilization we have to work very hard in spite of many conveniences. Inventors and scientists worked very hard also to produce amenities and conveniences like cars and aeroplanes and much more. It is a wonderful manifestation of all the activity that is stored in us in the form of energy. So in this sense you can easily understand how significant it is that action is born out of Brahma, out of the Supreme Reality. Otherwise how are we to know that it is born out of the Supreme Reality, the Divine Consciousness? It is Consciousness Itself which has assumed the form of an activity! Consciousness of talking is coming to me so I am talking; consciousness of listening is coming to you so you are listening to me. If you are not conscious then you would not listen to me. I will go on talking to you – my action, your eardrums, the vibrations in the air are all there – but if you are not attentive then you cannot listen to me. You can just see that the energy which is in abstract form, in the potential latent form, is hidden in me and in you, and that is the same Supreme Reality. Space is everywhere, it is one. In the same way, that Supreme Reality, that vast omniscient and omnipresent Reality, fills this entire universe, called Divine

Consciousness. Again, it is a name, but the most important thing as I have emphasized to you repeatedly, is Its realisation. It is in you and that is what you are. **Tat Tvam asi,** 'Thou art That', are great words of wisdom from the **Upanishads.**

There are nine examples given in the **Upanishads** which illumine these words of wisdom. One is about a lump of salt and the ocean. Formerly, the salt had a form, like a piece of stone or marble. The salt came from the ocean and when placed in the ocean it dissolves. Then you do not find the entity separate from the ocean – it has become the ocean itself. This lump of salt, which was outside the ocean once upon a time, assumed a name and form, a lump of salt. When placed back in the ocean it becomes the ocean; there is no difference. You cannot take the same lump of salt out again from the ocean. In the same way, if there is a puppet of salt which wants to find out the depth of the ocean, can it do so? By the time it will seek, and dive into, the ocean, it will become the ocean! And that is what we are – the salt puppet in the vast ocean of the Supreme Reality. We have come out of It just as a puppet of salt has come out of the ocean, but, when it attempts to find the depths of the ocean, the puppet is no more. And that is what is happening to us – we are trying to discover, to find out the Supreme Reality.

We often ask someone, "Are you doing something, are you acting – doing some work?" We speak about it so easily without understanding what an activity is in itself. Activity and inactivity are relative terms, there is nothing like absolute activity. When the absolute activity comes into existence it becomes rest – it becomes inactivity and that is why it is in this sense that Brahman, the Supreme Reality, is inactive. It is not that it is lazy, lethargic or there is inertia in it. There is a great consciousness in the Supreme

Reality, it is Consciousness itself. But then we say it is inactive because the activity is taking place in some limited form – in limitless where would there be an activity? Activity, for example, is in this body because this body is limited; it is working in limited space, so the activity is taking place in something that is limited. But with that which is limitless, omnipresent, all-pervading, in *what* will that Reality act – because there is no space left for that Infinite Reality. There is no space left, it is ALL in ALL. Just see – inactivity is not a drawback of the Supreme Reality. By nature it is inactive. That is why in meditation we become so quiet, because, at that time, we are coming closer and closer to the Divine Reality which is completely inactive.

Inactivity is not a term to be abused – we must remember it is Brahman who is inactive. When someone is inactive people always say, "Oh, you must work, must work!" And activity *is* good, because it would be death not to work – it is a dead body which does not work! A living body must work, it must exercise the limbs. It is necessary for us, it is an impulse in us which enables us to work but we must also know that when we do not act it is not something bad, or wrong. That is why sometimes you are supposed to be inactive when practising **Hatha Yoga** for example; after every **asana** in which there is a lot of activity, in which you manifest much energy, you do **shavasana**. You are the storehouse of energy so it is out of you the activity is coming. So you are Brahman – **tat tvam asiā** In you Brahman lives and out of that Brahman **karma** (action) is coming out. **Karma brahmodbhavam** – so beautifully you see in this world that activity is coming out of the Supreme Reality. When you manifest the activity it is an impulse in you, a motivating force, and as long as you and I are alive we are supposed to work. And **see** the manifestation of all this activity – big cities, art, temples, churches, idols – all of these and more have come into existence out of activity. If a human being had not been active then all these things would not have come into existence!

So, activity is not meaningless. It must not be underestimated. That is why in society activity plays a very important role – if a person is not active and dynamic he does not have a respectable position, even from a social point of view. So a person must be active, he must do some work. In India, parents seeking a husband for their daughter first find out if the man is working, and if he earns enough to look after a wife and children. They want to see if he is active, that he works, or is lazy and does not work – if so, then no woman in this country will marry him! So he must work. Why? Again the same idea comes that action is born out of Brahman, out of you. Because Brahman lives in you just as space lives inside and outside a pitcher. So Brahman is in me, is in you, in a small child, in an elephant, a lion, a tiger, an ant also, and in an invisible insect it is the same Brahman. The Self does not differ. It is the same Self. The Supreme is always One.

The Absolute Reality is One. We may call it by various names – the final reality is One. The Absolute Reality cannot be two. Plurality can be a manifestation and expression, but the Absolute Reality is One. Out of that One Supreme Reality, even in all different kinds of activities, Brahman is One. The full beauty of this verse was learned at the sacred feet of my master. It is not possible to translate the very deep meaning of the Sanskrit words into any language, and if the spirit of words is not translated then we cannot do justice to the fact itself, the original meaning. We see the action, apparent when it assumes some form. Either it appears in our hands, feet, brain, thoughts and ideas – it becomes visible, takes on so many forms, big cities, villages – all expressions of this active energy which is born out of Brahman. All this creation at large – stars, moon, sun, rivers, mountains – all have sprung out of Brahman, have been born out of Brahman. See how the principle of creation has been described in the **Upanishads**, in the **Bhagavad Gita** and the **Vedas**. It is the Absolute Reality seeking its expression and is appearing to us in the form of human beings – children, sons, daughters, husbands, wives. The beauty of the **Vedas** ! Their clarion calls say, **sarvam khalvidam brahma (Chandogya Upanishad 3.14.1)** – all that you see with your eyes is Brahman! The individual self is not something different from the Absolute. You are not an ordinary thing! That is why we say we are not just this body. It is of course a very important instrument – without it I could not talk to you about the Supreme Reality. This body has been given to us in order to realize the Divine Reality and if we fail to do so there would never be a greater catastrophe than that! If you do not realize the Divine Consciousness life has been futile. The Buddha, Krishna and Mohammed are great because they realized Divine Consciousness in their lifetimes.

Do not think that God is hanging somewhere or sitting on a throne in heaven! NO – it is He who lives in me and is talking to you, it is He who lives in you and is listening. Do not forget **that**. It is this which was realized by Buddha, Krishna and Christ. To Christ everyone was a beloved and a giver of love, even those considered to be low caste. If we only **think** of it! It is in this land, India, that consciousness has been born in the past, and it is our people who are forgetting. As in the land of Christ, people have forgotten Him out of arrogance, envy and jealousy. What harm did He do to mankind, I ask you? After all, He was a great lover, He loved. He said God is love. Do you think it was a great sin he committed by calling God love, by loving mankind, loving the poorest of the poor – the outcasts? In those times also, Christ was criticized for eating and drinking with the outcasts of society. Outcast people are also the children of God – in them God lives, but it is only the God-full eyes that can see this. "God is love", said Christ and He lived it from moment to moment. The difference between Christ and us is that sometimes we talk but do not live what we speak. He practised what He preached. He lived in the constant companionship of God. When His disciples questioned Him regarding His instructions to them to "go out and give the message of God and take nothing with you, not even a staff", they said, "but where to sleep, where and what to eat?" He told them, "Do not worry". He was sitting in the open, amidst lilies, and He said, "Consider the lilies, they toil not, spin not, and yet I say unto ye that Solomon was not arrayed like any one of these. If God so clothed the grass, how much more will He clothe ye! O ye of little faith!" These are bold words which can only come from a person who is divinely realized, who is in constant companionship with God. What inspiring words these have always been for me.

Do you think the God of Christ is different from the Brahman of the **Bhagavad Gita**, **Upanishads** or ***Vedas***? It is the same principle – **ekam sat** – the Truth is One. Christ gave an example to His disciples of an insignificant little flower, lilies born in the fields and watered and fed by divine waters falling from heaven. He took such an example to show His followers that the One who looks after innumerable flowers will be also caring for their needs. Christ's eyes were riveted on the lilies, eyes made of flesh and blood like ours. But what we see depends on the attitude with which we look. He saw the Divine Reality there and that is why His Realisation was perfect, complete in itself. Faith moves mountains.

Love all religions of the world equally, have equal respect for all of them. It is the same Divine Absolute Reality which exists in all the faiths and religions and that is why we are the children of the same God. The same Father, but we children are different – speaking different languages, dressing in different ways, having different skin colours, different mentalities – but inside we are all One. Realise that Oneness and this world would be so beautiful! If we realised this much it would be worthwhile to live on this Earth. It is only by this kind of attitude that this world can be transformed and people live happily without war and violence. So think of it, try to revive it in your heart and life. Even one person who is bold and courageous can move this world to do and dare!

Verse 16

एवं प्रवर्तितं चक्रं नानुवर्तयतीह यः ।
अघायुरिन्द्रियारामो मोघं पार्थ स जीवति ॥ १६ ॥

Evam pravartitaṁ cakraṁ nānuvartayatīha yaḥ I
aghāyur-indriyārāmo mogham pārtha sa jīvati II 16 II

> *One who does not follow in this world the wheel of sacrifice thus established by the Vedas certainly leads a life full of sin. Arjuna! Living only for the satisfaction of the senses, such a person lives in vain and leads a life of sin.*

evam – thus; pravartitam – set revolving, set in motion; cakram – wheel or cycle of the world; na – not; anuvartayati – follows; iha – here in the world; yaḥ – who; aghāyuḥ – living in sin; indriyārāmaḥ – satisfied, rejoicing, indulging in the senses; mogham – in vain; pārtha – O Partha! The son of Pritha; saḥ – he; jīvati – lives.

In this **sloka** Lord Krishna told Arjuna about the old traditional lore of sacrifice. The Lord Himself has set in motion this cycle of action or the wheel of nature for nursing, training, disciplining and elevating all beings at varying levels of existence in order to realise the **summum bonum** of life. Sacrifice is the Supreme, it is the law of life. The individual and the cosmos depend on each other. There is a constant interchange. The world is in progress because of this cooperation between the human and the Divine. So a person who does not follow the wheel of actions, who turns away from the path of his own religious sacrifices, lives in vain, lives in sin; he lives uselessly. A man who wants to enjoy the sensual pleasures can't escape sin. He hankers after selfishness, pride, pleasures and prosperity and causes sufferings to others. He is of sinful nature. He remains in the pit of sinful misery. That's why no one should forsake his own religion, the path of his own religious sacrifices. It is the only path that should be always followed whole-heartedly.

Verse 17

यस्त्वात्मरतिरेव स्यादात्मतृप्तश्च मानवः ।
आत्मन्येव च सन्तुष्टस्तस्य कार्यं न विद्यते ॥ १७ ॥

Yas-tv-ātmaratir-eva syād-ātmatṛptaś-ca mānavaḥ I
ātmany-eva ca santuṣṭas-tasya kāryaṁ na vidyate II 17 II

But the man whose delight is in the Self alone, who is content with the Self, who is satisfied with the Self, for him there exists no work that needs to be done.

yaḥ – who; tu – but; ātmaratiḥ – rejoices in the Self, devoted to the Self; eva – only, alone; syāt – may be; ātmatṛptaḥ – satisfied in the Self; ca – and; mānavaḥ – the man of knowledge; ātmani – in the Self; eva – only; ca – and; santuṣṭaḥ – contented; tasya – he; kāryaṁ – work to be done, duty to perform; na – not; vidyate – is, exists.

In the previous **slokas** the thinking was devoted to performing all actions with the Divine in mind. But now the idea takes a turn in the mind of Bhagavan Sri Krishna. He uses *tu* (but) and *tu* is only used to mark a change in thinking and to highlight the new way of thinking. So, He says, **yas-tv-ātmaratir-eva syāt**, which means the one who takes delight in the realisation of the Self, takes delight in the Divine Life, who leads the Divine Life, who has experienced the Divine in his life, who has realised Self, who is Self-enlightened, Self-awakened, and who lives in that consciousness for all the twenty-four hours. Take care, that's why this **tu** has been used in Sanskrit. It is not for anybody. It is for one out of millions who has realised the Divine and is an embodiment of Divine Life.

Such a one is a Self-realised soul, one who has realised his Self; according to Patanjali's **Sutras, kaivalyam** – the state the loneliness, and according to the Budha, **shunyata**, the state of voidness; both mean the same – the absence of all dualities and pluralities. That means he thinks that all and the entire universe is One, it has come out of monality – there is no plurality in his mind. He thinks that all are embodiments of God, and all human beings are the living temples of God. He sees it and he lives it. Such a person is a very, very distinct personality. In such persons we can take the example of Buddha, Rama, Krishna, Christ, Mohammed. Such persons do not seek anything for their own satisfaction, they are satisfied in the Divine Life itself. They have attained perfection which means that they have realised their natural state of consciousness. The terms used above are synonyms, but they are **only** words until and unless you experience it. The most important thing is to experience it. And yet, there is an aim, an idea, which Bhagavan Sri Krishna is putting in front of a Yogi with intensity and authority, arguments and explanations, as to what can be done and attained afterwards. Such a state of consciousness will arise in him. It is not a state of self-complacency, nor of gratification. It is the state of self-contentment. He finds himself in all, and he is one with all. He has realised the identity in all – with the poorest of the poor, and the richest of the rich, with the saint of all saints and the sinner of all sinners. He takes the sin of others upon himself like Christ. He comes to take the sin of so many and it is from that that he suffers.

The concept of sin is also in Hindu mythology and in Vedic religion, in a particular, definite and precise sense. In Sanskrit, for sin, we mostly use the word **pāpam**, and **pa** is the root which means to protect. That from which we defend and protect ourselves is called **papa** – we should not commit an activity which will lead to afflictions, complications and problems of life. So we try to avoid it, but **papa** is done out of ignorance. It is a mistake, a blunder, easy to make. If a person would know, then he would never commit a sin. He commits a sin only because he is like a little child – he puts his finger in the fire and gets burned. He doesn't know because he has not experienced in this life what fire is and all of a sudden he puts his finger in it!

Papa is like fire. Fire cooks our food but if in ignorance we touch it then of course it burns our fingers! So the same energy which can cook our food can also burn our fingers. It is the same thing with sin when it is done in a right way out of right consideration, and in a very just and spiritual way, then it doesn't harm. The action is the same but because it is done with great knowledge, understanding and love, it cooks our food. "Cooks our food" means it gives us creation, we create and the same activity, the same sin becomes the creation. And creation is a very great joy, life becomes immortal nectar. For the Self-realised person there is never any problem with right or wrong. But there are very few people who are realised and that is why the **yamas** (restraints on behaviour), and in particular two of them, are so important for those who are Self-realised. These are **ahimsa** (non-violence) and **satya** (truthfulness). Not to speak the truth, to speak lies, is deadly poison. We should take care of speaking the truth, and we should try to speak something only after we have sufficiently thought and pondered over it. There is a French proverb which tells us that we should move the tongue seven times in the mouth before we speak. That is so that we may not speak untruths, or violent truths, nor speak biting truths, or speak to offend others. So we have to be very careful to speak truth – it is a great art, it is not an ordinary thing.

Mahatma Gandhiji used to observe silence for weeks sometimes before he would speak the truth to improve and correct others. Self-correction is the best correction and it is never too late to do that. Even a very corrupted person who chants the name of the Lord with love and devotion will be purified, he or she becomes a saint. When the heart is purified then no matter what a person has done, all is forgotten. Such teaching from the **Bhagavad Gita** has given inspiration and hope to so many people. Mistakes can become a habit. Once a mistake is committed it should not be repeated. That's why there is a repentance for it in every religion. There are many examples of repentance and lives changed for the better in Hindu mythology and in the lives of great saints. We do not know when the turning point will come.

Many youths used to come to Gandhiji's ashram and confess their mistakes and difficulties, and afterwards their lives were transformed. It was such a great relaxation, all their emotions would subside and they became very normal. I think that ashrams, these religious places, are divine mental hospitals in which the remedy of all problems takes place very peacefully and lovingly. That is why, unconsciously, people – young and old – come to ashrams although many do not know or understand what ashrams are. But really, ashrams are experimental laboratories, at least in India – for thousands of years! Problems are removed so patiently, peacefully and quietly. But then, this idea should be there – that divine consciousness comes to all and sundry. That is assured, because everybody is a pure soul, everybody by birth is so pure, but it is out of ignorance in this world that she or he does not know what they are doing when they commit sin.

tasya kāryaṁ na vidyate – for one who has attained divine consciousness what work is there left? What work was left for Christ? But then if He was doing anything it was just for the sake of love for mankind. He was not doing anything for himself; that is why his work was only divine work. Then there was no duty for him; you cannot impose the same duty on Christ, or Krishna, or Buddha, as on you or me. They are completely liberated and it is in liberation that creative works are done, works which move and shake the world. The hand which rocks the cradle moves the world. And what moves? It is the Self, the **Atman**, the cosmic consciousness. It is this cosmic consciousness which has been emphasised in this seventeenth verse beautifully. It requires great contemplation, concentration and meditation. People teach us meditation but what is it we meditate upon? It is this, the divine life, which we talk about before meditation. Such a life we meditate on – it cannot be handed over in one week, or one month! It requires a whole life time, like this river flowing from Gangotri to Gangasagar, right from the source to the place where she flows into the Bay of Bengal. This whole life is continuously, constantly flowing day and night.

Mark at least, that Yoga is not for a moment, or a day, or a year. It is for the whole of life. The Yoga which has come to the western world is only touching the fringe. We believe that Yoga is like the blossoming of a flower – it is a natural, spontaneous blossoming according to divine law. All the roses on the same tree are similar but they are never identical. Even in the same flower, which petals will open when and where? Perhaps the bud does not know, how much less the gardener or we would know!

Yoga is like that in everybody. It is not exclusive to India. It was born in India, that's true. Every child in the heart of the mother is doing Yoga – the child is doing **yoga**, he is performing **garbhāsana**. This is one of the 84 **asanas**, a difficult one. Every child is doing it in the heart (womb) of its mother. And every child lies with head down and legs up, just like a tree. Roots go downwards. Life has changed outside but inside it is the same divine law taking place with the creation of a human being. Imagine! – the child is doing **sirsasana** for nine months almost! Yoga starts right in the heart of the mother – it is so divine, so spontaneous. Yoga is in our nature and it helps us to evolve. Nothing is imposed, nothing is forced – how can you force a petal of a bud to open? It will be damaged, being so soft and tender. And Yoga is like this. Great Yogis may not speak but just to look at them is Yoga. Everything about them is Yoga, they live in Yoga every moment. When we come into contact with such a soul immediately harmony is created, there is no confusion at all. All conflicts are resolved. If Christ or Krishna came in front of us today we would be in harmony, but they might be surprised and might not accept us; we are supposed to be their devotees but we despise and hate each other! Where is love for each other, like God? But, even then, if Christ or Krishna should come, we would be completely transformed in their presence. Yoga is explained so very beautifully and clearly in the **Bhagavad Gita**.

The **Bhagavad Gita** is a sublime text and directly affects our lives. That is why we study each verse, one by one, with great care. The teaching is so clear and prepares us for all walks of life. **Yoga** is for the classless society. It is a universal concept, a cosmic concept. It is the spirit which is more important, but when it is done in a form of meditation then it is still much better, and for that purpose the **asanas** are there. When we speak of the **Bhagavad Gita** it prepares us – prepares the mental atmosphere. It's a happening. You can't say, "I am meditating" or "I have meditated" or "I will meditate". It's just a happening and when it comes we do not know. Only when it comes, then you know! So, it is for the divine life we are aspiring.

Verse 18

नैव तस्य कृतेनार्थो नाकृतेनेह कश्चन ।
न चास्य सर्वभूतेषु कश्चिदर्थव्यपाश्रयः ॥ १८ ॥

Naiva tasya kṛtenārtho nākṛteneha kaścana I
na cāsya sarvabhūteṣu kaścid-arthavyapāśrayaḥ II 18 II

Similarly, in this world he has no interest whatever to gain by the actions he has done and none to be gained by the action that he has not done. He does not depend on all these beings for any interest of his.

na – not; eva – even, surely; tasya – of him, of that man; kṛtena – by actions done; arthaḥ – purpose; na – not; akṛtena – by actions not done; iha – here, in this world; kaścana – any; na – not; ca – and; asya – of this man; sarvabhūteṣu – in all beings; kaścit – any; arthavyapāśrayaḥ – depending for any object.

The identification, realisation, with the Supreme Self, means to have this cosmic universal consciousness, to become One with all. Bhagavan Sri Krishna is uttering this **sloka** from His point of view. He knows that Arjuna has not realised this state of consciousness because Arjuna is still an individual and is standing on the individual plane. Of course Arjuna is struggling hard for Self-realisation but it has not come to him. Bhagavan is helping him to realise what his real Self is. The conflict is there in Arjuna's mind, between the body and the Self. There is a rough awareness in Arjuna so far as Self-realisation is concerned. There is nobody in this world who does not have a slight awareness of the Self. There is awareness, consciousness, in everyone but it depends on the individual as to what extent he or she will become aware of the Self and to what extent he or she has identified with the Pure Self, which means to be in love with the Pure Self. Because it is only in love that you become one with the object of your love, it is pure identification when you love someone even in this world.

So this kind of identification is in Bhagavan. He has become one with the cosmos, the entire universe. Bhagavan is working because He is living in all, so He is working through farmers, labourers, teachers, lawyers, though all kinds of people. Such a person who has realised the Supreme Self already is doing work through millions of minds, hands and tongues! Whether he does some work with this body or not, he is performing work through so many bodies, through so many he is thinking. And compared to all that assemblage of activity he is performing, what is the importance of this mere body? There is little concern with this body, this individuality, this personality. **Naiva tasya kṛtenārthaḥ** – then with this body he works or does not work. It means that his selfishness is completely lost, his ego has merged into the Divine, become one with the Divine. So it is the loss of complete entity. Then for such a person there is no selfish end for which he is working or not working. Wherever the Pure Self is realised that state of consciousness becomes matter of fact. It is a matter of fact for Krishna; it is not happening for Arjuna who is the representative of individual self. **Naiva tasya kṛtenārthaḥ** is good and holds good for Sri Krishna because He has identified Himself with all. So, for Him if He does some work it is good, and if He does not work it is equally good. It is only one body which is not working but He is working through so many.

The person who works out of selfish ends is needed in society. After all, everybody cannot be completely selfless, so people work. This verse is for the person who has transcended the objective world, in which he lives in a transcendental state of consciousness. Then only can he declare that he has no selfish end to achieve. There are such people living in society, in complete Self-awareness – not one iota of selfishness remains. It is not abstention from work, it is not denial of activity – you must be very careful about this. Why? The Pure Self is everywhere, it is omnipresent and omniscient. What activity will take place in that? Activity only takes place in something which is limited, which has a name and form! And that state of consciousness of Bhagavan Sri Krishna is formless because it exists everywhere, just like the sky. What form is there in the sky? And yet the wind is blowing, the stars and moon are there, the sun is rising. All this is happening in the sky, so many celestial bodies are just floating in the heavens. They are there, activity is in them, but in the sky, in the ether, in space, there is no activity. See, these bodies are moving, the activity is inside them, but what about the sky? It will be only active in something where it is not. Still subtler than the sky is the Pure Self, much more prevalent and pervasive. Then where in the Self activity will exist? That is what our real Self is. We are just going back to It, all of us, consciously or unconsciously we are trying, and unveiling ourselves. We are trying to realise our real Self – this Self – because out of this Self we have come and into this Self we are going back. That is why people are disappearing – once upon a time your ancestors were living and today they are no more. My father, once upon a time I could see, touch, feel him and then all of a sudden he disappeared from the face of the earth.

We do not think, but the fact is there: appearance and disappearance is taking place in this world. Most people who realise this phenomenon of appearance and disappearance know the secret of life. **Avyaktādīni bhūtāni** – in the beginning all beings were in their unmanifested state of creation, they were not visible. Everybody, including you and I, are coming from this state of non-manifestation. Before the world, we were all invisible. From the state of unmanifestation I am coming, and it is during this short span of life I become visible. Hands, feet, limbs, everything appears but it is only this life which is spent with it. And it is with this body I am realising the world outside, realising everything. Only during this life of 50 to 100 years. Afterwards I also go to sleep, eternal sleep. This mystery is taking place – the only thing is that we are not aware of it. You will say why become aware of it, there are many people who are not at all aware – how does it concern us? People are eating, drinking, sleeping, enjoying life – they do not worry from where they have come and to where they are going. For them it is not a concern at all.

People come from different countries and then they go back to those countries. But is the real "coming out" taking place? Have they really come from America to India? Do they really come out from this earth and go back in to it? Yes, the body does. All this happens only on the physical plane of existence, but not on the spiritual plane. The body merges in to the earth – but only because it has come in to existence from the earthen element. But what about the Pure Self which hasn't come in to existence from the earth? The Self is not born out of the earth, like the body. So, it's only the body which fades away and when the body is faded, it has withered away like a flower and all flowers fade away towards evening. This body is like the petals – an appearance of a flower. In the evening, one by one the petals fall and are lost. The seed remains, it is not faded. It does not have the beauty of a rose but innumerable flowers, a chain of flowers, are hidden in just one seed. You sow it back in the earth and out of it, again, a plant just rises. But not out of the petal, the petal just merges into the earth, however beautiful it was. It was much more beautiful than the seed and that is why sometimes we do not care for the seed. When we eat a mango we leave aside the skin and stone and are not aware that in the stone (seed) is an endless chain of mango trees. The stone doesn't speak to us, but, sow it in the ground, water it, nourish it, and see it sprout. The seed of a banyan tree is small but it contains a series of latent trees. It is not so beautiful as the fruit or flowers of the mango tree but it is in this unbeautiful thing that the whole series of trees lies. People do not care, they just throw away the seeds without a thought. We use the pulp of fruits and don't care about the seeds. The most mysterious thing is completely neglected. It does not concern us.

So the Perfection, the Reality, is not known, the Awareness of the Reality has not come because our consciousness is just skin deep, limited. But realisation dawns upon them who know that in the seed of a banyan tree there are multitudes of banyan trees lying dormant, they are astonished; So many trees just in a seed, which is even smaller than a mustard seed! They become aware of the Supreme Reality in which the entire universe is existing and the future of the universe is lying dormant, their identification is with all – he or she is working through all, already. He or she can be excused and it is this that Bhagavan is speaking out of Himself. Arjuna does not understand because his realisation is still in the world of relation, in the relative world, in this world – in a small circle, and that is what happens to us. But such is not the consciousness of Bhagavan – Self is there, He has become

One with that Self. And we do not become that – ours is a great confinement, a great imprisonment.

Tell me, why is it that we are sitting in a common place? What is the common factor? The common factor is the Pure Self which has been realised by Krishna. Everybody has this Self. He or she is floating in the Self, in the ocean of Self just like a fish. Fish in the water and birds in the air. Air and water are the media. Air is not visible to the eyes and yet it is a very important medium for the birds – if it is not there can a bird fly? In the absence of water where will a fish move around? They need a medium. In the same way, this body has a still subtler medium than air, than ether, than space itself, and it is this medium which is the Self. Likewise the fish comes from the water; in water it is born and sustained, and in water it disappears. From outside, if you see it, it is such a different liquid, but it is the water which transforms itself into the form of fish, just as the bird comes from the air. Air is a very important substance, please note, and you will be surprised, too, how our bodies come out of this air element. Birds float, fly in the air, mostly they are floating. Observe kites and eagles – they make an effort and then just float, they become one with the air. They make no effort at all – such great unification and harmony with the air. In meditation too you become one with the soul so you can begin to float in it and you will go in all parts of the world actually, just like a bird. You are floating in the Pure Self in meditation and you are visualizing sometimes that you are flying in the sky. It is a state of consciousness.

For one who has realised this state of consciousness, this ethereal body, whether he performs some action in his individual body, or not, there is no selfish purpose either. And also such a person is not dependent – on whom would he depend? There is nothing to depend upon, it is all-pervading. There is no dependency! This kind of independence we all want to realise because that is our tendency, that is our instinct. The liberation of the soul is when you have identified yourself with the Supreme Self, just as in love you identify yourself with another body, with another person. These things are happening in day-to-day life but we are simply not aware. We worry for nothing – in fact there is nothing to worry about. All is here, All is there, All is everywhere. But we have a narrow outlook, we are just confined to fears, anxieties, ideas and illusions. But when we are torn away, when the shackles are cut asunder, at that time you are just like a bird hatched out of an egg – just see! Think of the wonders which are happening in this world and you will see what you are, who you are! "Who am I?" – it is not the small I-ego. Am I this body, this mind, this tongue?

You are the centre of this universe! But perhaps you simply do not know it. Please remember it, note it down. You are not only this body. I don't live in time and space, it is only the body that lives in time and space. If you think of time and space you will become that material time and space alone. People think they are conditioned by time and space – how can they be? Can you catch hold of Ramana Maharishi and pin him down like a butterfly and analyse him? Impossible! It is the body only which will be pinned, not his soul – and the butterfly is a soul.

There is nothing, only liberty, and pure liberty, and liberation. And before that you are a slave – of money, name, form, and of satisfying your desires. Do you want to continue this kind of life, are you happy, are you satisfied? If you are happy and satisfied then please continue – I am not obliging you to give anything up. It is your free will, you are absolutely free, born free, live free! Nobody can make you a slave. Freedom is your birthright! Those stupid fools who make you a slave simply do not know! You must revolt against those who want to imprison you. They are stupefying you, simply hypnotising you – they don't want you to realise your freedom. That is your birthright. You are living in liberty and you shall die in liberty.

Do not be stupefied by others, do not give up your real nature. These people may come and tell you that you are a man, a woman, an Indian, an American, all life they tell you the same. For practical purposes it is very good, but I have to speak the Truth because I am seeing it out of my own personal, individual experience. Then you will realise it and say it with the same gusto, the same courage – the same thing. As soon as you realise you become That. Realise your own Self! Only such a one can live without depending on anything. This is a clarion call from Bhagavan Sri Krishna. In His non-doing there is a doing, and in His doing there is a non-doing, because He has the silence of the mind when He is working. Others are working just like donkeys – work becomes a drudgery. Be free! Be fearless!

Verse 19

तस्मादसक्तः सततं कार्यं कर्म समाचर ।
असक्तो ह्याचरन् कर्म परमाप्नोति पूरुषः ॥ १९ ॥

Tasmād-asaktaḥ satataṁ kāryaṁ karma samācara I
asakto hy-ācaran karma param-āpnoti pūruṣaḥ II 19 II

Therefore, without attachment, perform always the work that has to be done, for man attains to the highest by doing work without attachment.

tasmāt – therefore; asaktaḥ – without attachment, remaining unattached; satatam – always; kāryam – which should be done; karma – action; samācara – perform; asaktah – without attachment, by doing work as a dedication to God; hi – because; ācaran – performing; param – the supreme, the highest; āpnoti – attains; pūruṣaḥ – a man, a person.

Tasmat means therefore, **asaktaḥ** means non-attached to the fruits of action, **satatam** means continuously and constantly – a person does work as an offering to God. Just as we offer the food and fruits, in the same way he offers his work and the fruits of his actions to the Divine. It is not negation of work for a **sadhaka** (a person who is moving on the path of Self-realisation) – Bhagavan Śri Krishna makes it very clear that he works continuously, incessantly. **Kāryam** means that which should be done as a duty. Our duty here at present, for example, is to do **satsang**, meditation, the recitation of the **Bhagavad Gita**.

When we pronounce this **Bhagavad Gita** in Sanskrit the first advantage is that our language becomes pure and clean, just as our body becomes clean when we take a bath in Ganga. And when we speak a clean language, then our thoughts and words become clean also. I see its effect on my mind also. I am just like you, there is no superiority over you! In chanting the **Bhagavad Gita**, pure feelings and ideas come freely, energy is renewed. Sometimes when we exchange ill words which inflict insult on others our energy is drained. It is not an easy thing always to be equipoised in the mind and speak a just language which is needed, and that, too, in a respectful, sweet and soft way. We have to take care speaking to someone that we do not inflict a wound. A word wound is not easily healed. When our mind is pure then naturally pure thoughts are there, and so words are pure, and when words are pure then action (conduct) is clear and pure. They become divine in nature because there is harmony in a human being – it is the same person who is thinking, speaking and acting.

If thinking, speaking and conduct are right then a person becomes right, and the people around him or her at that time would become right. I am trying at least to have right thoughts – and right speech comes and naturally right conduct follows. You see how nicely we disperse to our rooms in a very nice way, we are good, loving and kind to each other. So right conduct comes naturally from the two hours we spend each evening in meditation and chanting and studying the **Bhagavad Gita.** This is not an ordinary attainment! Most people do not have even that much – please try to see that! That is why life becomes so disturbed, confused, perplexed, unbalanced, and people are at a loss simply not knowing what to do. After all, we are human beings! We are not all perfect on the mental, verbal and physical plane. So being a normal human being we are likely to have an unbalanced mind leading to unbalanced conduct. These things move so fast in our lives and they can hurt someone as soon as the equilibrium is lost when we are not **yukta** (balanced).

It is not an easy task. Really, living is a very great art and it is nicely described in the **Bhagavad Gita**; how to live our lives day to day, moment to moment. And that can be done by anybody belonging to any faith, religion or country or speaking any language. We speak Sanskrit because it is our mother tongue and it is very sacred, and it is very melodious. It is pronounced as it is written – we cannot write it one way and pronounce it in another. In pronunciation and writing there is no duality, no gulf between them, no conflict in the mind also. The sound vibrations of Sanskrit purifies our mind and heart, so for this purpose we chant the **Bhagavad Gita**. We are not a priest, we are not pretending to be a preacher or a teacher. We are ordinary human beings, ordinary **sadhakas** trying to perform **sadhana**. **Sadhana** means to realise or to balance – we are trying to realise our own Self in our own humble way. There is something common in us, and there are certain differences, and the differences should be taken into consideration as much as the similarities. Sometimes religious teachers do not take the differences into consideration. Differences are not bad. There are different kinds of flowers and these different flowers make a bouquet. On one tree there are different kinds of birds singing, and there are many different languages.

So from the language point of view we create an atmosphere when we chant the **Bhagavad Gita**. We do not repeat it just for the sake of repetition like a parrot without understanding. We try to understand each word, its purport, its significance, and then try to live it in our life as far as possible. But it is not easy to practice living it – easy to think, easy to speak but it is difficult to practise in our life. Even I cannot do it sometimes, I am also a human being like you. I am sailing in the same boat as you and I know my imperfections. We are all imperfect in some way or another, somewhere, and we should try to realise these imperfections in our life and try to remove them by ourselves. I cannot indicate those imperfections in your life and I need not do it because that may not be nice on my part. When you find out yourself, then correct yourself!

The most important effect of chanting the **Bhagavad Gita** is that the mind becomes relaxed. You come here with respect and honour in your heart. In a short time have gained so much understanding, realisation and experience, even if you sit here in silence. For these two hours we become so harmonious, equipoised and balanced in our mind I would be happy to have the other twenty-two hours like this. We try, we may not always succeed but we try to live our practical lives the same. Here I speak to you very nicely but sometimes during the day it is not the same, it may change slightly. And that also hurts me. I always pray to God when I sit together with you, "Make me a humble instrument of your hands that every word I speak may be so balanced that it may not hurt, that it may give joy, bliss and happiness."

Asakto hy-acaran karma – asaktah satatam – We have to perform actions constantly but should not be attached to them nor to their fruits. When the fruit of action is offered to God, naturally there is no attachment. For example, in this small piece of work here there is no attachment. I do it with great love and devotion because I do it with all my heart, and I don't feel that it is a burden. It is a great work of joy for me. If this work would not be given to me then I would feel sad.

Of course we can't chant the **Bhagavad Gita** for all twenty-four hours. It is not possible, nor is it needed. We have to work with the rest of society – that is how practical life moves on – but we can retain that spirit of the **Gita** in our daily routine. Whatever the work may be it is our attitude which is most important. The approach is inward. It is the inner attitude which is transformed – from outside you remain just as you are. Afterwards the outside changes by itself. It is something like sowing a seed in the ground – the seed doesn't remain a seed, it becomes a sprout. It changes, it is transformed. Slowly it grows and becomes a small plant, then a tree, then comes ripe fruit. These **slokas** are like seeds which we are sowing in your heart and in due course you will see the divine effect in your life. They do express in some form afterwards as they did in the lives of great saints like Gandhiji and Vinoba Bhave. So in our humble way we are trying to do the same work. This is the significance of reciting the **Bhagavad Gita**.

Here, emphasis has been laid on **asaktah** – "**saktah**" means attached and "**a**" means not - and **satatam** means constantly, incessantly. **Kāryaṁ karma samācara** – which means work which should be done (you can call it duty). **Kāryam** means that work of divine love. Here **samācara** means 'do'. **Asakto hy-ācaran karma** – by being not attached, **param-apnoti pūruṣaḥ** – then he attains the Supreme, the **summum bonum** of life. If he has learned the secret of life, that he works for others, out of love for others, for doing good to others, then at that time they become the means of realising the Supreme Good, the Supreme Love in which you are always engrossed, in which you live. When it is attained then our life is instantly thrilling, that is the beauty of our life, but this consciousness doesn't come usually. During the daytime we are so very extrovert that we do not seize, arrest, capture it with our whole individuality, our whole personality.

Bhagavan Sri Krishna shows how to attain it. **Tasmād-asaktaḥ satataṁ kāryaṁ karma samācara** – Perform your daily duties in whatever capacity you are working, by being non-attached to the fruit of action. Bhagavan is teaching us the secret of **Karma Yoga.** Most of us are **karmayogis** most of the time and this **Karma Yoga** is to purify our minds and hearts. It is a very great aid. Without actions we cannot purify our heart and mind. If we do not act, do deeds, work, our mind will not become purified. We will become angry, annoyed, disturbed. How long can we live without doing work? Work is a necessity for a human being. If people will not work together then they will dispute, there will be ill words and anger. So instead of that, why not act in the spirit of **Karma Yoga** in your life, why not try it? This verse is so important from the point of view of **Karma Yoga**, as work is done in love constantly.

If you really love someone then constantly you like to work because he or she is in your mind. You want to please, and her or his pleasure becomes your pleasure! At the time of your action you are lost in love, all the time some fragrance like a perfume comes out of you. And you are always in that Presence, living sweetly, softly, kindly, gently. And then, absorbed in love, each action, gesture, movement, thought, word, becomes filled and absorbed in love. You see, this life *is* worthwhile to live – what do we need more than that? But it is not an easy thing, we try but don't always succeed. But never mind, after all we try over and over again and one day it happens that we become successful, that our life becomes balanced completely by omission or commission. If we can avoid hurting the feelings of others by omission or commission it is good. We should not be ruthless in our life. I talk to you so easily but do you think life is so easy? So when time is given to us over here it is for our self-observation – you can call it self-analysis – that we sit here together. Just try to confess to yourself – not to me. I don't need your confession – as I am confessing my own drawbacks and imperfections, so can you. It is a self-correction. If you are writing a letter, even a love letter, and if there is something not right in it, you correct it yourself. Why should your beloved come to correct it? You just correct it out of great love. Similarly, you just love yourself, so just correct yourself. You will see that self-correction is the best correction.

Bhagavan is saying not to be attached to the action nor to the fruit of the action, meaning there should not be selfish motives or intentions. You know this ego is the cause of all our troubles in all of us, including myself. This ego when it becomes superior spoils the game! We become victims of this ego. We will try to remove it, to rub it out. If there is an eraser, it is this kind of meditation or thinking and reflecting we are trying to do together. Then the mind becomes clean. So you can understand my speaking of the **sloka**, how important is the chanting of it. In this way we are trying to work with a team spirit and sit together in a friendly loving way.

Verse 20

कर्मणैव हि संसिद्धिमास्थिता जनकादयः ।
लोकसंग्रहमेवापि संपश्यन् कर्तुमर्हसि ॥ २० ॥

Karmaṇaiva hi saṁsiddhim-āsthitā janakādayaḥ I
lokasaṅgraham-evāpi sampaśyan kartum-arhasi II 20 II

It was only by works that Janaka and others attained to perfection. Thou shouldst do works also with a view to the maintenance of the world.

karmaṇā – by actions; eva – only; hi – verily; saṁsiddhim – perfection, liberation; āsthitāḥ – attained, strove to attain; janakādayaḥ – Janaka and others; lokasaṅgraham – protection of the people, guidance of men; eva api – only; sampaśyan – having a view; kartum – to perform; arhasi – thou shouldst, ought.

Bhagavan sees the mind of Arjuna, and sees that there is a conflict in it and wants to help him so that he may be able to resolve the conflict. What is the conflict? It is that Arjuna wants to escape from the duties of his life. He thinks that his duties are so horrible and violent (fighting a war), but if the path of knowledge – **Sankhya** – is so easy to perform then he can meditate, sit, discuss mental problems and study the scriptures. Why suffer so much to perform his duties as a warrior, a **Kshatriya**? Arjuna wants to follow the path of least resistance – it is a human tendency to do that. But without Herculean effort the Self cannot be realised. Up to the moment a person becomes Self-established he should not give up his duties, he has no right to do so. If he will not perform the duties of his life, then there will be retrogression, or repression, or recoil, or withdrawal, or even a fall is even possible. If, due to hardships, or out of weakness, fear, anger, or hatred, one withdraws from duties, denies them or escapes from them, then fulfilment will not be there. Completion and perfection are not gained – Self-realisation will not be there.

It is only by passing through the hardships of life and through the furnace of afflictions during the lifetime that one comes to realise the real significance of the world. Without entering the world, for example, do you think you would be able to realise the world? Even if parents and teachers advise children about the sufferings and afflictions and consequences of worldly life, the children cannot afford to escape life. We may try to escape the Self, but Self does not escape us, it is always in front of us. It is always there until we face It. Ordinarily we want to escape a difficulty in life, but escape does not help. And it is this kind of withdrawal – inner immaturity and unripeness – that Krishna is seeing in Arjuna, the right evolution is not there.

I remember a French mother who used to say, "Look here, if you are pampered and worshipped by people, then your natural evolution is not there because you begin to think yourself superior, and a kind of ego appears and you want to have a superiority complex instead of Self-enlightenment." So we are deceived, we think that we are realised because we are worshipped, pampered and praised by others. But that has **nothing** to do with Self-realisation. Self-realisation is an entirely different thing – only the person can know whether she or he is realised or not. From outside it is very difficult to know because there is no sign externally. Many people did not even know who Krishna actually was; they saw only the appearance and behaviour – a play – in His life. The same with the Buddha. Great souls are only known after they have passed away, because they behave just like an ordinary person, like us!

So we think that they are just one of us, until they reveal themselves; otherwise, they will be shut up and closed. People will look with open eyes but even the person closest to them will not know! And that is what happened with Christ; He was not known by His closest friends and companions because He was eating, walking, talking, living with them. A very normal human being in a way, and yet, there was something extraordinary, abnormal, about Him which only He knew, or a person with very sharp eyes, or another enlightened person, knew.

There is a possibility that only a Self-enlightened person can understand another such person. There are certain attributes, of course, which appear with enlightenment and which are not commonly found in an ordinary person. For example, lust is not there. Purity of heart and mind is there, no desire is left, all desires have come to the state of cessation. If there is the least desire remaining then perfection has not been attained, completion has not occurred. **Samsiddhim** means the accomplishment, perfection. Accomplishment is a word but what does it mean? An accomplished person does not have any desire because all desires have been fulfilled in Self-realisation. Desires will never be fulfilled before Self-realization. That is the beauty of Self-realisation and why people want it; there is not the least trace of desire. Lust is not there. Is it not a great emancipation not to be a victim, a slave of lust, over and over again? Even up to the last day of their lives, sometimes, people cannot control themselves, even old people find it hard. Over and over again they become sad, unhappy, and afterwards they repent, and yet they cannot control, cannot dominate themselves. Only when Self-realisation is present there is a complete merger of lust in the Pure Self, the blissful state of joy. Lust only comes to them when the joy of Self-realisation is not there. Starlight fades in the greater light of the moon, moonlight fades in the greater light of the sun. Stars and moon are there in the sky during the day but we cannot see them because of the brightness of sunlight. And Self-realisation is a million times brighter than the sun!

We are striving for such a Self-realisation, and after it, this body, like petals, just withers away. The flower is there and bees come to collect nectar for the purpose of cross pollination. The flower is beautiful to look at, it attracts many birds and insects – they do not know that they are the agents of Divine creation, that pollen grains are left on the wings for cross fertilization. On fruit trees as soon as the fruit arrives the blossom falls by itself because the work of the blossom is over. Flower petals wither away by evening as soon as the seed comes. It was destined to protect generations of plants and trees. See how conscious is Divine Life! **Nothing** is unconscious in this universe, that is why consciousness is universal, cosmic. We are filled with consciousness. We can never be invisible, we cannot hide ourselves. No work can be done in secret! We cannot hide ourselves from the eyes of the Divine. A person who has realised the Self will never do any evil – from whom will he steal when he has realised the Divine is everywhere? About whom will he think evil? From whom will he listen to evil? Where will he see evil? Self is the Light of the Light!

We simply do not know it. We think we are so poor, with nothing to eat, no shelter, clothes, money and building; we think that we do not have riches and prosperity, name, fame and glory. For a Self-realised person all these things are futile, meaningless, insipid; they have no significance. That is the beauty of Self-realisation – if we could only realise that Self. Obviously the **Upanisadic** thinkers have given thought for century upon century about Self-realisation and passed on their findings. See, you are in such a land as this! If you want to understand Christ, come to India – many people believe that He came to Kashmir. I would not be surprised, caravans travelled from the Near East to India on trading missions. To learn about Self-realisation the masters travelled to many places, near and far. We do not know how many doors we have to knock on before we come to Self-enlightenment. It is not so easy. It is only after the crucifixion of the self (ego) that one can realise the Pure Self. If the ego has not been placed on the cross it is impossible to realise the Self.

Buddha said that the cessation of desires is the cessation of miseries. And if this does not come to us, see how poor we are! We may be a multi-millionaire, an emperor, but if Self-realisation has not come to us, if we have not realised the Divine Life, then what are we? Empires and great leaders have come and gone. Such power they had and now they are lying down in books, in biographies! We do not consider them as the incarnation of God like Krishna, see! Did Krishna or Christ have an empire? Their empire is in the heart of mankind. We read Krishna's work, His teachings. His empire is limitless because He is One with Divine Consciousness, so we have His wisdom and knowledge today.

It is this Divine Life that Bhagavan is speaking of in this twentieth verse. **Samsiddhim** means the perfection, the Self-establishment. Arjuna was in conflict, he did not want to take part in a ferocious battle. Krishna knew that Arjuna's nature was like this: that even if he would be asked to realise the Self he would not do so – he would fight! That is why many people outwardly become monks and saints but inside them that instinct of a warrior is there. So even among themselves they fight. That is why there are fights in the name of religions. Do you think that in the real name of religion – Divine Consciousness – in the omnipresent, omnipotent, omniscient consciousness, there can be any fight at all? Christ said the kingdom of heaven is within you – you are That! Can anyone say this unless he has become one with this Divine Consciousness? What is life without it? It is **this** Consciousness, which should be realised inside our temples, mosques and churches.

If this is forgotten all these buildings become meaningless, they are only stones because the Reality is lost. It is only a skeleton when the spirit is not there. You can wash a skeleton and it can be very white – but the soul is not there, only bones. Similarly with a place of worship; if the priest has not realised the Divine, then this building is like a skeleton, lifeless, without a soul. Self-realisation is very difficult. It is easy to earn money, glory, name and fame and because of these glamorous things the world has forgotten. In you and Christ there is no difference – your Self and the Self of Christ are one and the same thing. The difference is only in the body, in the mind. We are not aware, we are unconscious, so we are suffering. We think that we are poor ignorant sinners. Christ said, 'hate the sin, not the sinner'. Such beautiful teachings He gave.

"I am a seeker of Truth," you may say. But what is that Truth? It is this which is Truth, and when this Truth is realised Life shines, it radiates. Such a person cannot be hidden, even after death. Even today people are discovering Christ, discovering Krishna. All over the world people are chanting and dancing in the name of Krishna. We saw so many happy people in western countries chanting His name, faces shining with happiness. You may say they are no longer Christian but what difference does it make if they are not Christian, if they become Krishna conscious? After all, Krishna Consciousness and Christ Consciousness are one and the same thing from the Divine point of view.

It is this Divine Consciousness which Sri Krishna is speaking of in this twentieth verse, and this consciousness has been realised by King Janaka. If you have attained the perfection, if you are Self-established, then for the benefit, the welfare, the good of others, for the world-integration, you should work. If you are not realised, then work for that attainment, but you must work. Even after Self-realisation one does not cease to work. In fact one begins to work in the right way, just like Krishna and Christ. And how much they have worked for century upon century! After 2000 years another Christ is not born; after 2500 years another Buddha is not born; and after 5000 years another Krishna is not born. Imagine, they have worked so much! So much potency and light are in them.

It is for such perfection that Bhagavan Sri Krishna is asking us to work, telling Arjuna not to become lazy, lethargic. He is inspiring him, telling him he has to work: "In work is thy right but not the fruit of action." An incarnation, a prophet, a saint, does not work for a reward; He works out of great joy, for all. And that is what He is asking us, to work for the sake of love of God, of Divine Consciousness. Do not aspire for anything less than that, and do not stop until you have reached the goal!

Verse 21

यद्यदाचरति श्रेष्ठस्तत्तदेवेतरो जनः।
स यत्प्रमाणं कुरुते लोकस्तदनुवर्तते ॥ २१ ॥

Yad-yad-ācarati śreṣṭhas-tat-tad-evetaro janaḥ I
sa yat-pramāṇaṁ kurute lokas-tad-anuvartate II 21 II

Whatsoever a great man does, the same is done by others as well. Whatever standards he sets, the world follows.

yad-yat – whatsoever action; ācarati – does; śreṣṭhaḥ – the best, the superior, leader; tat-tat – that; eva – only; itaraḥ – the other, inferior; janaḥ – people, man, a person who follows him; saḥ – he; yat – what; pramāṇaṁ – standard; kurūte – does, upholds; lokaḥ – the world; tat – that; anuvartate – follows.

Bhagavan Sri Krishna in this **sloka** speaks about the responsibility of a great soul, a **srestha**. A **srestha** is a great man who knows the reality about the world (body, etc.) and the Self, the absolute. It is not an easy thing to become a great person or a great soul. It is a great achievement. Afterwards it is a very great responsibility, because a great soul is followed by millions of people. People have a tendency to follow. Whatever that great soul does is done out of contemplation and reflection. He does not do something all of a sudden, without understanding, he does not do anything unconsciously, nor without practising it in his own life first. He speaks through his deeds. An iota of practice is better than tons of theories, and that simply means that whatever a great soul teaches he lives. Great souls are born all over the world, like Rama, Krishna, Christ, Buddha and Mohammed.

A person who is Self-established (of whom Bhagavan has spoken in previous verses) is Self-realised. But Self-realisation is not meant only for one person. It is meant for all, it is open to all. In the absence of Self-realisation life is a burden, a drudgery, a slavery, an imperfection. Self-realisation is the message of each verse – Bhagavan Sri Krishna teaches, points out, in each **sloka** that Self-realisation is so difficult. It is easy to talk about but it is difficult to practice, and to live in that state of consciousness always. Not at all an easy thing to live in that Transcendental Consciousness! So a self-realised person, male or female, casts a great influence on the bulk of society – like Ramakrishna Paramahamsa for example, or Ramana Maharishi. Both were very simple in their living, appearance, conduct, behaviour, conversation, movement – in all aspects of life. In fact, after Self-realisation a person becomes very simple, and his language also becomes very simple. There is no complication even in the language used. The more we are Self-aware the more we are simple in thought, word and deed.

Bhagavan Sri Krishna is that simple and He is speaking very simple things to each of us, about the simple facts of life. And speaking about Self-realisation which comes not only to Him and Arjuna but to everybody, because everybody is Self-realised, only the awareness is not there, is not conscious. So many problems are just created in Self ignorance. Sufferings, insurmountable sufferings come only because the person is not Self-aware.

There are the celebrated words, too, of Bhagavan Buddha. "Be a lamp unto yourself," he said 2500 years ago. What a simple teaching! Buddha was born into a royal family as you know; he marries and then leaves His family when renunciation called. He leaves His newly born son – who would not like to see glimpses of His own son? It is the father who is born in the form of a son. See, it is very strange at this juncture to think of the father siring his son and then leaving after the birth! A sense of detachment (**vairagya**), the spirit of renunciation, appears to Gautama (Buddha) and He leaves home. For seven years He stays in the Himalayan mountains. He realises the Self. What austerities He performs, such a hard life He lives, and yet after Self-enlightenment He comes to the conclusion that that austerity, that suffering of the body, was not needed. And yet He was the outcome of it!

What did He do all during those seven years? What He attained we could call **Boddhisattva** – awakening of that Existence, which always exists. All is appearance and disappearance, this is the play which is going on. You appear here and then after two hours you disappear. The same way in the world, people appear, from non-appearance they come, and then they disappear and we do not see them any more. There are no footprints left. Just as birds leave no trace in the sky so also human beings come and go. All beings in the beginning, in the origin, are unmanifested, says Sri Krishna in the second chapter of the **Bhagavad Gita**. In between the two (arrival and departure) you appear, all of us do, for varying lengths of time, and then we depart.

Have you thought about it? Gautama did, and for seven years at that time. For us it is difficult even to think for a moment of such a great Reality from which we are coming and to which we are going. It is strange, this Eternity, this Existence, which people are afraid to realise. They are frightened and do not want to talk of it because it is hard, it is difficult to realise that Unity, Eternity, Cosmic consciousness, Divinity of Life. I have told you many times these are just words, try to see the significance that they correspond to, try to transcend the words to That which is beyond the words, which the words are indicating. Try to see That in life, and not only intellectually – it is not an intellectual comprehension, it is the whole of your individuality, the whole of your personality, with the whole of your existence – just as the Buddha did. He seized it, was absorbed in it, lived, walked, ate, drank and slept in it. He did everything in this state of consciousness; that is why He is called Buddha. In Sanskrit Buddha means the Awakened One, the One who is awakened to the Divine Reality, to Divine Consciousness. Ordinary people are awakened to the external world so much – see how people are just running and rushing around as if they have lost something! Do you see it? Have you not done it? What are we running after? Illusions, and that is what we are beginning to realise. It is of this that Ramakrishna spoke to his devotees. This consciousness hardly dawns upon us towards the end of life! The end of life is too late, our body is collapsed, it is dilapidated, lethargic, doesn't function properly. When there was strength in the wings we were completely forgetful, we didn't fly in the open space – we were like a musk deer, running and running and running and running! When the musk appears there is so much energy in the deer and he runs to seek the scent of musk everywhere. And from where does the fragrance come? All the time it is in his own abdominal glands!

We run in the world like a musk deer. The whole of our lives, sometimes, we run after money, material possessions, name and fame; even for creating children – nourishing them, bringing them up, but then, towards end we are disillusioned because one day we have to be disillusioned. That is what Shankaracharya is thinking in his commentary on each and every step. That great disciple of Ramakrishna, Swami Vivekananda used to say, "You are hypnotised by the world, de-hypnotise yourself!", and he realised the Self before the age of 39 years. By whose blessing, whose grace, and whom did he follow? By Ramakrishna, who was a **Shrestha**, a great soul it means – a **Mahatma**, always in Divine Consciousness. Who would not like to follow such a one?

That's why Bhagavan Sri Krishna is saying in this verse, whatever a great soul does, acts and performs, other people will follow. If Ramakrishna had not conducted a divine life, his own, how would Narendra (Vivekananda) have followed it? And so many since then too. Words are pregnant with meaning, they are not devoid of significance. Every word used in the **Bhagavad Gita** has a significance. **Shrestha** is not anybody – Shankara is one, Ramakrishna Paramahamsa is another. **Paramahamsa** means supreme swan, living in the world but never touched by the world. Swans live in water yet water never pierces their wings. In the same way the world does not touch great souls. Otherwise, everybody is touched by the world. Most people are like crows. You might have seen a crow taking a bath in water, it is just drenched everywhere! After, it is very difficult for him to fly until his feathers have dried! A crow's wings are not impermeable to water. Swans can dip into water and then take off to fly immediately and there is not one drop of water on them. They circle around and then plunge into the water just as a Yogi plunges into meditation. Krishna, Rama, Buddha, Christ, Mohammed are great swans, great souls. They are sresthas. They have a great influence on the mass of people and people follow them. It is a great responsibility. When we sit for a moment in their presence and reflect upon it and begin to just live it even for a moment, we are absorbed, we take the Divine Love and swim in a pool of peace. Such is the presence of a great soul. Whatever standards he sets, others follow and attain peace, become happy and lost in meditation. It is a great responsibility to be a **srestha purusa**.

Live such a life, wherever you are; it doesn't matter whatever your profession or mode of life may be. All that is needed is to imbibe this spirit, this state of consciousness, this realisation, this experience. Only then are these words lived, become significant and full of meaning and potency. Seize them! Catch them! Arrest them in your heart and let them be completely absorbed by every pore of your body, heart, mind and soul.

The great seer Yajnavalkya said to Maitreyi: "**Ātmā vā are draṣṭavyaḥ śrotavyo mantavyo nididhyāsitavyaḥ**", which means: First of all **draṣṭavyaḥ** – see the Self **atman** everywhere, in what ever you are doing. Then **śrotavyaḥ** – listen to the **atman** through the great saints and the holy scriptures. Do not just leave it after hearing, that is what people do. They hear with one ear and take it out of the other. Then comes **mantavyah,** to think about the Self, the **atman** which is in every human being potentially.

Then at last comes **nididhyasanam**, which is full of significance and up to this stage people do not go. After listening they leave. Finish! The further process is not done, work is unfinished, you need patience and perseverance which is nine-tenths of life. Realisation and experience is unaccomplished, imperfect and we remain on the path faltering and falling down. **Nididhyasanam** means continuously and constantly, incessantly, for a long time, up to the end; to discover, to unveil, to contemplate and to meditate. People do not like to go up to this stage.

They become impatient like a child who has sown a seed in the ground and does not water it, who then cries that nothing has come out of the seed! The mother will tell him to wait for some time, just wait. You have sown the seed of love and devotion, but it cannot be grown in a day, or overnight. It takes its own time and has its own course of evolution. As the mother told the child, you, too, should have patience and perseverance, and then the sprout will come.

Verse 22

न मे पार्थास्ति कर्तव्यं त्रिषु लोकेषु किंचन।
नानवाप्तमवाप्तव्यं वर्त एव च कर्मणि ॥ २२ ॥

Na me pārthāsti kartavyaṁ triṣu lokeṣu kiñcana I
nānavāptam-avāptavyaṁ varta eva ca karmaṇi II 22 II

I have, o son of Pritha, no duty, nothing that I have not gained, and nothing that I have to gain, in the three worlds; yet, I continue in action.

na – not; me – my; pārtha – o pārtha; asti – is; kartavyam – to be done; triṣu lokeṣu – in the three worlds, heaven, earth and the regions in between, corresponds also to physical, vital and mental plane; kiñcana – anything; na – not; anavāptam – unattained; avāptavyam – to be attained; varte – am; eva – also; ca – and; karmaṇi – in action.

All beings perform actions in order to attain something. The Lord also performs actions but, although there is nothing which should be done or attained by Him, He incarnates for the welfare of others and performs actions for the protection of the good and for the destruction of the wicked and for the establishment of righteousness. Incessant activities are done by the Lord. You can see in his incarnations as Rama, Krishna and others. Lord Krishna had nothing to gain or lose in the **Mahabharata** warfare; yet he engaged on the battle field of Kuruksetra as the leader of the Kshatriyas, because the Kshatriyas are duty-bound to give protection to the distressed. The part he played in it was far more than those of all the other characters put together.

He is the controller of all other controllers. Everyone is under His control. He is above all regulations of the revealed scriptures, yet He does not do anything that violates the scriptures. There is no one greater then Him and yet He performs His duty. As the Lord performs His duty, he never abandons it, so also we should always perform our duty so that we may reach God easily. If we do not perform our duty we remain deprived of God-realisation. So all the time we should try to perform our activities for the welfare of the world. Can you imagine, if the Lord and the saints did not perform their duty, the people would also follow their paths, they would become indolent and heedless and would perform forbidden actions.

Verse 23

यदि ह्यहं न वर्तेयं जातु कर्मण्यतन्द्रितः ।
मम वर्त्मानुवर्तन्ते मनुष्याः पार्थ सर्वशः ॥ २३ ॥

Yadi hy-ahaṁ na varteyaṁ jātu karmaṇyatandritaḥ I
mama vartmānuvartante manuṣyāḥ pārtha sarvaśaḥ II 23 II

For, if I did not engage Myself in action unwearied, men would in every way follow My path, o Arjuna.

yadi – if; hi – surely; aham – I; na – not; varteyam – engage in action, continue; jātu – ever, at any time; karmaṇi – in action; atandritaḥ – unwearied, vigilantly, untiringly; mama – my; vartma – path; anuvartante – follow; manuṣyāḥ – men; pārtha – o partha; sarvaśaḥ – in every way.

Lord Krishna is extraordinary in His conduct. In everything, whatever He is doing, He is a great example, the greatest authority to mankind. He is incarnated in the world to set an example to other people. The world is an educational institution where we have to learn how to do good to others, to work selflessly without attachment to attain liberation. Therefore to keep the balance of social welfare for the progress in the spiritual life, traditional, Vedic family usages have been meant for us human beings. Lord Krishna established and followed them also. Even in the **Srimad Bhagavatam** it is said that He was performing all the Vedic duties at home and out of the home as prescribed in the scriptures for a householder. Such rules and regulations are for us and not for Him and yet He is following them. Why He did so he explains in the next verse.

Verse 24

उत्सीदेयुरिमे लोका न कुर्यां कर्म चेदहम्।
सङ्करस्य च कर्ता स्यामुपहन्यामिमाः प्रजाः॥ २४॥

Utsīdeyur-ime lokā na kuryāṁ karma ced-aham I
saṅkarasya ca kartā syām-upahanyām-imāḥ prajāḥ II 24 II

If I should cease to work, these worlds would fall in ruin and I should be the creator of disordered life and destroy these beings.

utsīdeyuḥ – would perish, uprooted; ime – these; lokāḥ – worlds; na – not; kuryām – would do, perform; karma – action; cet – if; aham – I; saṅkarasya – of confusion, intermingling of castes, of the admixture (of races); ca – and; kartā – author, creator, agent; syām – would be, shall become; upahanyām – would destroy, would ruin; imāḥ – these; prajāḥ – beings.

In this twenty-fourth verse Bhagavan Sri Krishna is putting an ideal in front of people. It is a great responsibility to live in this society. If I do not work due to indolence, if I do not put effort in activity, then I cause harm in society. It is a violence not to work, especially when we are capable. Our moral sense obliges us to work, and in fact there is an energy in us, in potential form, which wants to seek its kinetic expression in the form of work. It is healthy to work. There are those who cannot work due to illness or some handicap and they can be excused. A normal healthy person works, one cannot be without work. If a person will not do right work in society then he will do wrong work – what else will he do with the energy ?

Let us understand Bhagavan's statement objectively and rationally. He says, **utsīdeyur-ime lokāḥ** – which means these people shall be uprooted, there will be disorder in society if I shall not work because they follow Me. I have put an ideal in front of people and if I cease to work due to indolence then people will not know what to do. And that is what sometimes happens – some people start to work with a great ideal and due to some drawback, some imperfection, the work is given up. If the head of an ashram, for example, would not work, what would be the condition of the ashram ? It will be in disorder, the organization of the ashram will be lost, so it is very important that the head of an ashram, guiding the destiny of it, should work in the right direction. When we follow certain traditions it is not because we are fanatics, or we want to observe some narrow outlook; these traditions have been the experiences of ages, they have been handed down to us for our benefit. If Bhagavan Sri Krishna puts an ideal of activity before the people, then **He** must work, and He is working.

He is asking Arjuna to work. Arjuna has some kind of confusion in his mind. We are all confused, you know, in our lives – it is usually the case! In that confusion we sometimes do not know what to do. As normal human beings, in our confusion if we do not work, at that time we can be excused and accepted, but we must want to come out of that confusion. And so we take the right decisions in our life in order to guide the destiny of our own selves and the people who surround us. It is not always easy to take the right decisions once the wrong decision has been made and its consequences manifested – it is difficult to come out of it. That is why when performing an action we take care as to what will be its result. So it is a great responsibility to place an ideal before people as has Bhagavan Sri Krishna who is followed by so many in India and elsewhere. He says, "Look here, if I would not work due to indolence what will happen to this society? There will be confusion and disorder, and people will perish." **Perish** is not a proper translation of utsīdeyuḥ – it means people shall be uprooted from their place, from their natural disposition.

I am sitting here talking to you, and thinking, which is a mental activity, an important activity which should precede action. A wise man does an action with knowledge; and a fool does an action without knowledge and sometimes there are heinous consequences for himself and others concerned. So it is in this sense I shall be uprooted, not in my proper place. If I do not act, do not work, then I shall be restless. Activity gives stability to a character. Activity is necessary for a human being, as long as he is eating food and has normal health, then it is good that he acts. A normal human being, unless and until something happens to him, does not cease to act – walking, talking, eating, doing something. So activity is very natural and spontaneous because it is an outlet of our energy. For that purpose we read and study here – it is very important work that we do. We do not study for some examination, or to prepare a paper as we do in colleges and universities. And yet we are doing something which is valuable and important for your good and the good of ourselves, and for others at the same time. So the question of **utsīdeyur-ime lokāḥ** in our case does not arise – people will not be in disorder.

On the contrary, there is a kind of order as people sit here quietly and peacefully. **Utsīdeyuḥ** will be only if, for example, I do not come and sit for satsang, saying, "I'm too tired." Even if I am tired I come because I consider this an important activity whereby I come into contact with people, become like a thread inside a rosary (**Mala**) which binds the beads. Once I told you that the beginning of spiritual life is to think of others. To think of others at every instant, every moment, at every juncture, as to what will be the consequences of my action upon them. This has to be taken into consideration. If we are observant and analytical about our thinking, speaking and conduct, then there is organization in our own lives, there is harmony. There are some people who are not in harmony with themselves. You may have seen them – they are confused and there is hardly any relevance in their conversation, so it becomes difficult to talk to them. So it is good that such a person takes a rest for some time. He or she sees so many things, it is so difficult for him or her to assimilate and put these things in order inside. It takes time.

It is for this purpose that we come to an ashram for a kind of retreat, taking the consciousness of our own self – body, mind and soul together. And that is the purpose of coming here to sit in meditation peacefully, and not to be in a tearing hurry. Because in haste sometimes things are spoiled, but if you have the patience and perseverance, and if you act in peace, then things are improved. They go from good to better, and from better to best. We have experienced this in our life and so we are saying it to you. But it is entirely up to you to accept it – **if** it suits you, **if** your reason allows you. If your understanding does not allow you, then you can just leave it, we will not mind. After all you are free, you are an individual, you are a free person.

Freedom is a great responsibility. It is a double-edged razor. If we do not use our freedom in the right sense of the term then we cut ourselves, just as a double-edged razor, if not used with care, will inflict a wound on our body. In the same way with freedom also. We can lose it. Sometimes I think I am free if I do whatever I like – but it is not like that! Jean-Jacques Rousseau said, "We are born free but everywhere in society we are in chains." You may not like what Rousseau said but there is an element of truth in it. We could live in the forest as primitive people are doing – there are still Sadhus living in caves in high mountains who do not depend much on society – but we are living in society. Being social beings, it is our moral sense which asks us to do something for others as others are doing for us. The food that I eat, for example, hundreds of people work for it, thousands work for the clothes that I put on my body, and so many people laboured to produce the materials and build this house in which I live. We can think about the labourers who work from morning to night – what is their life, do they have peace, are they satisfied? I try to think about my fellow beings around me when I have time.

So when Bhagavan says here that **utsīdeyur-ime lokāḥ** – "these people will be in confusion, in disorder, if I shall not work" – not only if Krishna will not work, but if you and I will not work in our individual capacity, and if we will not contribute to the total activity – there will be some discrepancy, some trouble. If I do not take the initiative in doing certain things due to indolence, then I shall cause harm in society, then it becomes a violence. So a person who is capable of working is supposed to work and should work, because the energy has got to be exhibited otherwise it will go in wrong directions. So you can understand that this activity of which Bhagavan is speaking, is very important, and is an ideal He is placing before us. We should try to do the same thing in our lives so that in order to have collective activity we contribute something to mankind, so that disorder is not created in society. It is in this wider context that Bhagavan is speaking. He is saying that he must work no matter what the circumstances. He has a very great and dynamic personality. We don't only call Him Bhagavan to worship Him – He is working very hard for the emancipation of mankind, which we would come to know if we sought deeply into His life. This teaching that He gives to Arjuna is so important and useful for us also.

Whatever work you do, you know the responsibility of earning a living, but what about the collective life of the world ? Bhagavan says, "If I do not work, then **ime lokāḥ** – these worlds or nations – will collapse". He does not speak of pride or arrogance – He is denying inactivity. In the case of Arjuna, he must act, must take initiative and do something and not become a lop-sided personality, sitting quietly without doing anything. Telling Arjuna is telling all of us because it is the kind of common knowledge we should possess, that "inactivity will bring world confusion".

Verse 25

सक्ताः कर्मण्यविद्वांसो यथा कुर्वन्ति भारत ।
कुर्याद्विद्वांस्तथाऽसक्तश्चिकीर्षुर्लोकसंग्रहम् ॥ २५ ॥

Saktāḥ karmaṇyavidvāṁso yathā kurvanti bhārata I
kuryād-vidvāṁs-tathā'saktaś-cikīrṣur-lokasaṅgraham II 25 II

As the ignorant men act from attachment to action, o Bharata, so should the wise act without attachment, wishing the welfare of the world.

saktāḥ – attached; karmaṇi – to action; avidvāṁsaḥ – the ignorant, the unwise; yathā – as; kurvanti – act; bhārata – Bhārata, Arjuna; kuryāt – should act; vidvān – the wise, the knower of the Self; tathā – so; asaktaḥ – unattached; cikīrṣuḥ – wishing, desirous of; lokasaṅgraham – the welfare, guidance of the world.

Ignorant men are highly motivated to act by their matter – inclined impulses and longing for name, fame, prosperity and sensory happiness. Lord Krishna warns us again and again against egoistic attachments in our life, since attachment is the root cause of all human sufferings. Working because of an attachment becomes a necessity and when that necessity is not fulfilled, man experiences misery. He makes his life full of worries, sorrow and tragedy. The wise man on the other hand has no personal motive. He has detached himself from worldly pleasures, his aim is to find joy in working for good, for the welfare of others. Out of compassion for the ignorant he ceaselessly works. He sets a right standard for all who are lower on the ladder of Self-realisation. He automatically leaves an impression on the ignorant people who are attached to action whether it is clearly seen or not. Not only human beings but also animals, birds and plants are influenced by his feelings and actions.

Verse 26

न बुद्धिभेदं जनयेदज्ञानां कर्मसङ्गिनाम् ।
जोषयेत्सर्वकर्माणि विद्वान्युक्तः समाचरन् ॥ २६ ॥

Na buddhi-bhedaṁ janayed-ajñānāṁ karma-saṅginām I
joṣayet-sarva-karmāṇi vidvān-yuktaḥ samācaran II 26 II

Let not wise man established in the self unsettle the minds of ignorant people who are attached to action; he should set others to act, himself performing his duties with devotion.

Na – not; buddhi-bhedam – unsettlement in the minds; janayet – should produce, create; ajñānām – of the ignorant; karma-saṅginām – of the persons attached to actions; joṣayet – should engage; sarva-karmāṇi – all actions; vidvān – the wise; yuktaḥ – balanced, steady; samācaran – performing, acting.

The word "integration" means to bring or to come into equal participation. There are some people who are easily integrated into society, who easily adapt themselves. Other people do not feel at home, they are disintegrated, they cannot combine or easily feel the harmony of others. It is a great problem – it's not always an easy task to be integrated. People have different interests and ideas and to live an integrated life with others is not easy. So Bhagavan Sri Krishna says, **na buddhi-bhedaṁ janayet,** which means do not sow the seed of conflict in the minds of unwise people, those who are not Self-realized. A Self-realized person is always integrated in himself or herself, and consequently is always integrated with others also. It is the same Self that is living in all human beings. A person who is dissatisfied with himself is also dissatisfied with others. We simply do not know it, we are unaware or unconscious of what is happening within us. So for that purpose we require great vigilance.

First of all when we get up early in the morning we try to integrate our own self which may be in a state of disintegration due to certain incidents, happenings, that have passed by. So we get up early and prepare ourselves and sit for some time, if possible peacefully, and meditate. In meditation there is an integration. You might have seen great differences in your travels to different places, cities; a great difference of cultures and civilizations, so we cannot deny that we are having great differences, diversities of life. But there are also great similarities; if there were no similarities we would not be able to sit together. Sometimes the similarities are more and the dissimilarities are less, and vice versa. No two persons are identical in this world – it is not possible. Names and forms, appearance, complexion, eyes, nose, etc., all these are different from individual to individual. It is very important when we are seeking a unity of life, an integration in this disintegrated world, that we take into consideration the differences, and we just don't rule them out. Take them into account and admire the different tastes, ways of living and thinking and language. So with all these apparent differences is it possible to find something which is undifferentiated, something unitary, a union of life, some kind of union within?

Yes, when we sit in meditation a union within is discovered. It is this approach which has led us to meditate together. And that is why meditation in Sanskrit is called **Brahmasamadhi** – **Brahma** means divine, and **samadhi** means meditation hence divine consciousness or divine awareness. That divine awareness is in everybody irrespective of caste, creed, faith, religion or language. You will understand more and more that meditation is a great wonder which has been discovered in all nations, in all faiths – somehow or other they know how to meditate in their own way. That's why there are so many kinds of meditation taking place today. All have a similarity – how to find harmony and peace so that we may live together, can coexist. Which can be a difficult thing even in a family sometimes, and how much more so can it be in the big world outside!

Meditation has given us the thread of beginning, how to start. So we have found the secret of coming together, whatever your name, form, language, faith, appearance, and so forth and so on; so that at least we may come and sit together for a moment of silence, to rest, relax and be peaceful, and to become aware of and take account of ourselves for a moment. When you come from outside naturally there are influences of all kinds. So to be able to come to yourself, to remove those outer influences from your sight, and to sit with others and be knitted as one is a very soothing experience. I like it. We all like to sit together in peace and in harmony in a loving way. All the better if we like to speak afterwards and exchange views in sensible and useful conversation, which may help and guide us to our destination. It is good that we can sit gently and softly together. We have a very nice definition to describe one who knows how to sit in a meeting in the company of others, one who knows how to conduct himself – **sabhāyāṁ sadhuḥ sabhyaḥ**. When you are alone you can do as you like, but when you sit with other people you have responsibility to think of them. And that is what we try to do here, think of others. So, ***sabha*** means meeting – the one who knows how to sit in a meeting and behaves gently and lovingly. In our individual capacity we behave in one way, and collectively we behave in another way.

There are some people who are ordinary – emotional, unaware and ignorant. The great majority of humans are of such like. There is a very small minority who are Self-aware, and Self-awareness does not breed selfishness. When a person is Self-aware then there is awareness of all that surrounds him because the Self does not only live in this body. It is in all. My life depends on everybody. I am not all alone by myself. Self-awareness means to look towards others with respect to what I can do in order that they progress in their life too, to render my services in the humble capacity in which I have been gifted. And everybody is gifted in some way and everybody can help everybody. Helping is very important, nobody can exist by himself at any age. That is why when we live together we coexist and have a sense of cooperation, a sense of mutual sympathy which comes out of spontaneous love; without thinking, the gesture of help comes. Bhagavan says for those people who are called **ajnani**, means those who are unaware, unconscious, "Do not sow the seeds of conflict". Do not split their mind and do not call them by any such names – "fool, stupid, crazy". We would not like to be called the same. Do not flatter, but at the same time do not say, "You are a donkey, a fool." Even if someone is ignorant do not call him ignorant but try to understand his ignorance. He or she is ignorant due to circumstances, may be because of their upbringing or lack of education. There are many kinds of ignorance. We become inert in our thinking sometimes, the mind doesn't think for days at a time. Call it depression, laziness, sadness or any name – these are the passing moods of life which come to everybody. An ignorant person does not know what to do with that circumstance. A wise man knows that sadness, depression, anger, hatred, jealousy, malaise, and envy are all due to Self-ignorance. With Self-ignorance all these things come. With Self-awareness you will see that all ignorance will disappear. Like lighting a lamp in a darkened room – immediately the darkness is dispelled. In the same way, when there is enlightenment of the Self, such a person is called wise. Wise is not a person who has read many books. Through books you have information but wisdom does not come from books alone. More than book learning is needed for Self-awareness.

When I speak of self I do not mean the ego. I mean the Self that is in you, that is a very subtle consciousness which enables you to be aware of your surroundings. The Self which brings you from a distant country – if you had not been aware of India you would not have come! As soon as the idea comes you become aware. From such a long distance mere awareness brings you here! You go through all the procedure of coming to India. But how? When the awareness came! There are people here in India who do not know what are our States and Provinces, what languages are spoken. They are just confined to their little self and they are living in it like a flock of sheep. But in you the idea came that there is a country like India, and with your initiative and courage you undertook this adventure and came to India. You are not only aware of me and I of you, but I am also aware, sitting here, of happenings in your countries. Bhagavan Buddha called it **alaya vijnan**, i.e. the abode of awareness, the abode of knowledge. These are words, but try to see the significance of them, and transcend the words and try to understand the things corresponding to them.

So, this **alaya vijnan** is in all of us, even in a small child. This awareness is not an ordinary consciousness. Some people are settled in it, it is very refined and acute and sharp – to them this awareness comes easily and quickly. This awareness is very subtle, and they can be aware of so many things together at a time. It depends upon their development, upon their evolution. On the other side there are people who are called in the language of the **Bhagavad Gita**, **ajnani**, meaning unaware. With regard to such unaware people who are engrossed in their own activity, we must not split their mind, calling them ignorant. Sympathize with them, do not sow the seed of conflict in their mind by telling them that they should not be attached to the fruit of their actions. There are people who are very deeply attached to the fruit of their action – they would not even **think** that there would be a possibility of working in the absence of reward (fruit) of their action. The idea simply would not enter their mind. They would ask, "Why should we work if we do not get a reward?" The high state of realization which comes to the wise man does not come to everybody! How to live it, how to practice it, and how to work?

Bhagavan Sri Krishna shows a very simple way and that works with Him in the small things of life, preparing food for example, reading and studying together, gardening. In many things you can find that you share the activities of an ordinary person. And also, if he or she needs the rewards of action that reward should be given – it is not to be discouraged. See, for example, labourers who are working building the homes all around. They have families, they work hard because they have an expectation that they will get a reward, their wages. The question of their working without reward simply will not arise because their children will starve! So, for them, we allow them to work and we have no disregard for their work. Perhaps we may not work exactly like them but we can arouse them, and we can, for example, do **satsanga** and we can study. If they do not study we cannot abuse them or criticise them for being ignorant. Do nothing like that! On the contrary, if possible, we are to be Self-possessed and at the same time to help, and not sow the seed of conflict in their mind, "You are wrong, you are on the wrong side", and so on.

Action is of course a necessity but there are people who are attached to it and cannot give it up because they have been working all their lives. The difficulty is that when such people become old, and the body is weak, they find they cannot work with the same zeal as before. They then do not know how to occupy themselves and are bored with life. They do not know, perhaps, that they can sit quietly and meditate. It is only a highly realized person who can face his or her own Self. Most of us are trying to fly away, escape from our own Self because it is very difficult to face. And even if you want to close yourself for a day in your room, all alone, you will find how difficult it is! So, you can understand that for those people living without Self-awareness, living like ordinary people, we should not put conflict in their minds. **Joṣayet-sarva-karmāṇi** – Employ them in work according to their gifts, according to their mind; **vidvān-yuktaḥ samācaran** – that he (**jñanin** – a realized person) will also work with them and integrate with them. We cannot teach only through words, we must also live and work together; only then is it possible that they will understand our teachings. That cannot be done by sowing the seed of conflict. In this verse Bhagavan Sri Krishna has again given us an important teaching.

Verse 27

प्रकृतेः क्रियमाणानि गुणैः कर्माणि सर्वशः ।
अहङ्कारविमूढात्मा कर्ताऽहमिति मन्यते ॥ २७ ॥

Prakṛteḥ kriyamāṇāni guṇaiḥ karmāṇi sarvaśaḥ I
ahaṁkāra vimūḍhātmā kartā'hamiti manyate II 27 II

All actions are performed in all cases by the modes of nature. He whose mind is deluded by egoism thinks, "I am the doer."

prakṛteḥ – of nature; kriyamāṇāni – are performed, being done; guṇaiḥ – by the qualities, by the modes, by the gunas; karmāṇi – actions, activities; sarvaśaḥ – in all cases; ahaṁkāra-vimūḍhātmā – one whose mind is deluded by egoism, bewildered by false ego; kartā – doer; aham – I; iti – thus; manyate – thinks.

Prakrti, i.e. the nature, is that state in which the three gunas **(sattva, rajas and tamas)** are totally in a state of equilibrium. When the equilibrium is disturbed creation begins and the body, senses and mind are formed. The three **gunas** or attributes of nature are the highest, **sattva**, endowed with purity and light, the second, **rajas**, characterised by passion and activity and the third, **tamas**, marked by ignorance, gloom and inertia. They execute all the activities of the material world, like birth and growth of bodies and plants, the flow of the rivers, etc., as well as actions like seeing, hearing, drinking and eating. All these activities are carried out by the mode of nature. These **gunas** (modes of nature) are present in all creatures in different proportions and impel an individual into action and his actions will be characterized by the gunas in him.

There are two types of person, one who works selflessly for the welfare of all, who does not work for the fruits of actions, and the egoistic person, who does not think of others. Both working on the same level may appear to be working on the same platform, but there is a wide gulf of difference in their respective positions. The person who just works for himself thinks that he is the doer of all actions. He forgets that in reality the **gunas** of nature perform all actions. Deluded by the ego, he identifies the Self with the body, mind, the life force and the senses and ascribes to the Self all the attributes of the body and the senses. He feels elated when he stumbles on success and feels depressed when he meets with failure. He does not see that nature is doing all and that he is misrepresenting and disfiguring nature's works to himself by ignorance and attachment. He is incapable of distinguishing between the action-ridden nature and the actionless Self. He is enslaved by the **gunas** and therefore mastered by pain and pleasure, happiness and grief, desire and passion, attachment and disgust. He has no freedom.

If he could perceive nature as the executor of all activities and enjoyer of all the fruits, then he could stand aside and enjoy all the happenings, success and failures alike, as a pure witness and discharge his duty unattached at the same time.

Verse 28

तत्त्ववित्तु महाबाहो गुणकर्मविभागयोः ।
गुणा गुणेषु वर्तन्त इति मत्वा न सज्जते ॥ २८ ॥

Tattvavit-tu mahābāho guṇakarma-vibhāgayoḥ I
guṇā guṇeṣu vartanta iti matvā na sajjate II 28 II

But, O mighty-armed, the knower of the truth of the distinction between the qualities (of nature) and their operations becomes not attached (to actions) knowing that qualities operate amidst qualities.

Tattvavit – the knower of truth; tu – but; mahābāho – o mighty-armed; guṇa-karma-vibhāgayoḥ – of the divisions of qualities and their functions; guṇāḥ – the qualities; guṇeṣu – amidst the qualities; vartanta – operate; iti – thus; matvā – knowing; na – not; sajjate – becomes attached.

Tat means "That", and **tattva** means "That-hood", the **Atman** or the Divine, because for ignorant people the Divine is very far away. In fact it is not far away, it is the closest reality because it is Truth. In the English version *tat* is translated as Truth. Truth, beauty and love are the attributes of the Divine. Gandhiji always said, "for me truth is God". So this translation is an appropriate one for an ordinary person to understand, but it is the literal translation I am giving. **Tat** is a pronoun and from **tat** comes **tattva**, an abstract noun which means "truth". **Tattvavit – vit** means "knower", so the knower of the Truth, the Divine or the Existence. You should not be confused with the words even if there are several terms used. It is an addition to our knowledge that we understand what words have been used in the past for indicating one universal and cosmic consciousness.

Tattvavit-tu – **tu** is used by Bhagavan Sri Krishna to mark a contrast. In this case the contrast is with ignorance because He spoke of ignorance in the previous verse – **ahaṁkāravimūdhātmā** (verse 27) is an infatuated person. The knower of the truth is not infatuated, as soon as he knows the truth then the infatuation disappears, ignorance does not remain. Just as when you put on the light darkness is dispelled. **Mahābāho** means "O, long-armed" and refers to Arjuna (in India long arms are a symbol of knowledge, wisdom and heroism, for example, Lord Buddha, the Healing One, had long arms) and Sri Krishna is telling him, "As you have conquered the world outside so try to be a hero of the spiritual life." Recall that Arjuna is a mighty warrior who does not want to fight a war against his kin. The **Mahabharata**, of which the **Bhagavad Gita** is a part, is not a treatise on war. Gandhiji said it is a spiritual war, a war between right and wrong, and this war still continues in our heart and mind and sometimes even up to the last moment we do not know what is right and what is wrong. Really, it is not an easy thing to go on the spiritual path. There are difficulties, ups and downs, separations and depressions, and we are all trying to live the Divine Life as far as possible in this world.

Guṇa-karma-vibhāgayoḥ means **karma** (actions) are the outcome of the three **gunas** (attributes, constituents) which are **sattvaguṇa**, **rajoguṇa** and **tamoguṇa**. **Guṇā guṇeṣu vartante**, means that these three **gunas** are acting in **gunas** themselves and the Self remains uninfluenced. There is no activity in the Pure Self, activity takes place in the material world. **Iti matvā na sajjate** means such a person does not become attached to the action and consequently not to the fruits either. He knows the secret of action and, thus, is not attached to it.

Bhagavan is saying: "O Hero (Arjuna), on the contrary, the knower of the Truth of the distinction between constituents of **prakriti** (nature) and their operations does not attach himself to work knowing that constituents occur amidst constituents." The wise man knows that activity is the function of ***prakriti*** **(gunas, which are her constituents)** and since it is her work it is her domain, her empire which she is governing and she is all in all. It is the monarchy of the **prakriti** where the **purusa** does not interfere, does not poke his nose. Wise man means **purusa** and **purusa** means "wise man". Attachment means to interfere, to poke your nose into the domain, into the affairs of **prakriti**. A **purusa** just witnesses the **prakriti's** actions and when you are a witness you don't act. So, **purusa** has been called inactive, not in the negative sense of the term, but he is vigilant, he is a supervisor. It is the task of the body to act and to work and this part of both men and women is **prakriti**, but women are considered the greater part of **prakriti** because they are by nature very active and dynamic.

By nature **prakriti** is active. In Sanskrit **prakriti** is feminine gender. Women work, are active and dynamic and that is why they are also called **Shakti**, incarnation of energy. In India we see women working everywhere; even when they become very old they continue to work. Women all over the world work hard – they **are** energy. It is in this sense that **prakriti** is active because she is **Shakti**. And **purusa** is more a spiritual and divine consciousness, gracefully living in paradise.

We say in our country that "where women are worshipped and respected, Gods live", but now that has become "only a scripture, only poetry". Still, there are noble families where women are worshipped. That is true Indian culture; feminine nature has been given importance here in **prakriti**. A **purusa** is more of a witness, he is not attached. But **prakriti** is attached, but without attachment the work would not be possible. They are sometimes like opposites – how to reconcile them? That is the question!

We must know why conflict exists in our mind. Conflict exists between the two principles in us – **purusa** and **prakriti**. An ordinary person, an ignorant person, simply does not become aware about the domain of **prakriti**, about the periphery, the circumference, of **prakriti.** You can't say that it is illusion – that it is nothing. No! It is something very important, we are living in it. At least we are witnessing it. Even the **tattvavit** (the knower of the Truth) witnesses it; when he becomes the knower of the Truth he does not rule out this **prakrita** (produced by nature) world. He becomes a pure witness to it, he becomes a seer, an onlooker. Attachment, wrong identification is not there. Usually people identify with outside happenings and not with the inner life. For a short time when we sit here together, some kind of magnetic principle operates – we are like needles which are magnetised as soon as they come into contact with the magnet – temporarily, during the time of **satsang**. And then the magnetic influence disappears we become just the nature – **prakriti** – and we identify with that, whereas before we were trying to identify with the Self which is the real nature of all of us. There is a duality, but **tattvavit,** the knower of the Self, knows he has become Self-aware by the practice of meditation.

In fact, what do we meditate upon? We meditate upon our own Self. So, when we meditate upon Self we become Self-like. We begin to have the attributes, the qualities of the Self. Self is eternal and unchanging, immutable, permanent, omnipresent, omniscient and omnipotent. So, when we come to the realisation of the Self, then all these attributes come to us because they are the very nature of the Self. **We become aware of them**. That is why our knowledge is increasing day by day, increasing not in the sense it is growing but rather we are revealing the real nature of our Self, and becoming aware of it.

So, the knower of the Self becomes a witness and is not affected by the **gunas** acting in us and their manifestations and expressions in the objective world outside. The **Gunas** are the expression and manifestation of **prakriti** and are within her domain. What is happening in **prakriti** is not happening in the Pure Self. As the knower does not attach himself to **prakriti** he remains uninfluenced, unaffected and not infatuated. A Yogi is in this equipoised state of consciousness – he is established in the Self. A person established in **prakriti** would become like **prakriti**, that is why people are restless. If I would go and identify myself with the world outside I would become like that. It is completely in the hands of each one of us to choose his or her path. You stay here in satsanga for a couple of hours each evening and then return to your room, and next morning you can go to the city and be like people in the world, you would be restless and disturbed. But it is better that you go into the world outside with understanding and knowledge so that you may not be affected. A Self-aware person will not identify himself with the world outside, but those who are not Self-aware may not know that there is a way out because they identify so completely with the fast, dynamic life of the world and all its attendant pollutants; this is **prakriti**.

So, we are not to identify with **prakriti** (nature) which is limited, but to identify with **purusa** (Self) which is limitless. We want to live in harmony and peace, we want to coexist, we want to live an integral life, and for that purpose we are studying the **Bhagavad Gita**. It can be useful to you and me today, as it was for Gandhiji in his daily life. We would not read the **Bhagavad Gita** if it was only a history or treatise on a war 5500 years ago! We are not students of history, we are students of Divine Life!

Verse 29

प्रकृतेर्गुणसंमूढाः सज्जन्ते गुणकर्मसु ।
तानकृत्स्नविदो मन्दान्कृत्स्नविन्न विचालयेत् ॥ २९ ॥

Prakṛter-guṇa-sammūḍhāḥ sajjante guṇa-karmasu I
tānakṛtsnavido mandān-kṛtsnavinna vicālayet II 29 II

Those who are misled by the modes of nature get attached to the works produced by them. But let no one who knows the whole unsettle the minds of the ignorant who know only a part.

Prakṛteḥ – of the prakrti, of nature; guṇa-sammūḍhāḥ – persons deluded by the gunas; sajjante – are attached; guna-karmasu – in the functions of the qualities, of the gunas; tān – those; akṛtsnavidaḥ – of imperfect knowledge; mandān – the foolish, the dull-witted; kṛtsnavit – man of perfect knowledge, the knower of the All, one who is himself a knower of the Self; na – not; vicālayet – should unsettle.

Bhagavan is speaking about the knower of the whole and the knower of the part. You see, a bud blossoms into a flower for a certain purpose, a certain function to be fulfilled. It is destined to do something in creation. It is also beautiful to look at, it has fragrance, and it has nectar which attracts the bees. If a flower would not be beautiful we would not be attracted, if it is not fragrant we would not be pleased, and if there was no nectar the bees would not be busy. So, in the evolution of nature all these different qualities of a flower are playing important roles, whether we know it or not, because nature is moving from imperfection to perfection, from something that is unaccomplished to that which will be accomplished.

Unaccomplished and accomplished are not contrary, not opposed to each other. Rather, they are a complement to each other. In the same way, in the whole world – if you will look at it – if flowers would not come, then from where would the seed come? As soon as the seed comes the petals wither away one by one without making any noise. It is surprising that the greatest works of nature are being done in great peace and silence. So slowly do these petals fall that if you sit beside them you will hardly hear any noise as they fall to the ground. Then, all petals accumulate on the earth and only seed is left. The bud is destined to be a flower and it blossoms so harmoniously, so perfectly. Each petal in itself is a perfection; it is a part of the whole you see, but it is the part that makes the whole – a part is not something in opposition to the whole. A petal falls and you see there is an incompletion, you feel there is something lacking in the flower if even one petal is not there. They are arranged and organised in such geometrical perfection, similar to each other yet each is different! Sometime, please, when you have time and your mind is quiet, look at the wonders and miracles that are taking place in this beautiful and loving nature which gives us teaching that all the books in the world cannot give.

Nature is an open book – all that we require is for our eyes to be open and to have a keen observation. That is, to have a keen observation with awareness, with understanding, and then the mystery of nature is revealed to us. Then the flower does not remain silent, it speaks something to us but only to the one who has the ears to hear it. Flowers have their own language – it is not any language like our own – but it is only for those ears which are tuned to it, are used to it, can listen to it. It is a great joy to listen to the beautiful symphony taking place in the world outside. It is worth living. Prior to hearing that symphony we are unaware, without understanding, and that is not the joy of life. It is not worthwhile if we live as if this life is a burden, a great suffering, something which is suffocating – a choking process. It is very difficult to come out of great moments of depression. Sometimes it seems there are no signs of life, and yet there is something wonderful in us. Inspiration comes! Again we become alert, alerted to our own Self, and to the objective world – the world outside, which is also the expression of our Self. But it is only later on that that is realised. And we all have to realise it one day or another – that margin is left up to you, to all of us.

But the fact remains that whether a flower knows it or not (whether we know it or not), every blossom ends in a withering away. Every Spring ends in an Autumn, and perhaps if our eyes are gifted then the Autumn is as beautiful as the Spring season. Spring is gay, it is loving, gushing joy. How beautiful Mother Nature becomes. All becomes crowned with diadems and gorgeously dressed. Looking at it you are astonished – who is decorating the beautiful trees? Where are the hands which decorate them so wonderfully? We see the function but we don't see the hands! When you want to paint a tree or flower there are hands involved – a person, canvas, brush and paints. In nature you don't see the painter, canvas, brush and paints anywhere. A painter is inspired to paint and becomes a creator. When he looks at beauty it goes in his eyes, heart and mind, and then that which he feels deeply is expressed. Anything that is deeply felt is bound to be expressed. What wonderful creations great artists have given us – they echo in our hearts and we dance with great joy.

Joy dances, joy sings, It is not the poetry or the song or singer, it is the happiness, the joy, the oozing out of the heart that dances! "For oft, when on my couch I lie; In vacant or in pensive mood, They flash upon that inward eye; Which is the bliss of solitude; And then my heart with pleasure fills; And dances with the daffodils." Nature's Poet, William Wordsworth dances with daffodils. He took time to look at the daffodils. There are people who afford the time and they can see, for them there is a complete identification with nature. It is the bliss of solitude – that inward eye which Wordsworth wrote about. I am most alone when left alone! The poet danced with the daffodils – when you actually begin to dance the poetry flows from you.

What is this life that we sometimes live? It is living like a corpse! Is that worthwhile when you can have so much joy and happiness with the bare necessities of life? Abundance is there in nature – life is such a great boon given to us providing we can understand its beauty. There can **never** be anything more valuable than life itself, it is the most precious gift. Life "outside" and life "inside" are one continuous whole. What a person sees inside is what he sees outside, he creates an atmosphere by his presence. If people are sad, gloomy, miserable, envious, jealous, hating, angry, disturbed, confused, they will create exactly the same thing outside! But a person who is free (it is our birthright to be completely free) is happy and contented, self-contented. *Not* self-complacency please – these are two different things. But contented with few possessions. It is not worldly possessions alone that make us happy. People hanker and run after possessions, doing so much to attain them, and they simply do not know how many of them they can do without. Still, people pursue possessions, running in a vicious circle, and sometimes they may reach a point of no return. Why? Because they are not realising the Self. They are seeing the part but are not seeing the whole. What to do in such a case?

Bhagavan Sri Krishna says we should not disturb those who do not see the whole. They won't accept the whole and we should not ask them to accept it, you can't force them. You can't criticise a bud – it is **akṛtsna** (incomplete) but it is still beautiful in creation. Just see! Why do you want to disturb the bud because it is not a flower! She is going to open herself according to her own law and nature. Sometimes in haste we want to open the petals with our fingers – do we know what a great injustice and disservice we render to the bud? No gardener would open a sensitive bud with his fingers. He knows that according to the law of nature, a bud will blossom into a flower and the flower will give place to a seed. Is an unconscious, ignorant law playing a part in nature? **No**, nature is at work and she has her own laws. She is conscious about what she is doing.

Everybody is going on his or her own course of evolution, everybody is experiencing a phase in that evolution. Who are we to judge what is happening in anyone? If the flower is incomplete, let me first understand that it is still incomplete. I cannot abuse or criticise the flower because, if I do so, the flower will not be changed. The flower has to play its own role. In the same way, I think, every individual, however imperfect he or she is, is playing his or her role in order to fulfil something. Everybody is trying for fulfilment. Some people are advanced, others are not so advanced. Should we rule the latter out, blast them away? Should we become annoyed and disturbed, should we confuse and disturb them? Usually when we are disturbed we disturb others, and when others are disturbed they disturb us – the traffic is both ways.

A sense of tolerance is needed. As we sit here together a kind of knowledge and wisdom is dawning upon us, so why not learn from Bhagavan who says of such people **prakṛter-guṇa-sammūḍhāḥ** – they are infatuated. Even if people are deluded, if they have illusions, what would you do? Is it possible for you or me, all of a sudden, to remove his or her delusions? And who has not had illusions, been deluded? Was I not deluded once upon a time, and how can I say that I will no more be deluded in this life? And even when we are in the illusion it is so beautiful to look at it. Therefore when we are out of the illusion then we should look at it as a beautiful painting. Why should we despise it, blow it away, criticise and underestimate it? We should not say, "Pooh, it is nothing", because had it not been there then how could I have been able to pass my life? What is an illusion for a knower of the Self is a reality for another person in the world. But even if I say that it is maya do you think that those who are in the illusion will accept what I say? They will not, because for them it is a reality, it is part of their life, and you can't condemn them, nor the illusion that is taking place, however ephemeral it may be in character! I know that Self is a bliss, an ecstasy, and enlightenment, but for a person who has not realised, what does it mean? Self-enlightenment, Self-awareness are words, beautiful words, but without experience they are only words I am speaking to you. You'll say, "Oh yes, this gentleman thinks very nicely," but what do they mean to you unless you experience enlightenment, which is the most important part of life?

Those who are not ready to hear of the Reality will not listen, but with great love, like Bhagavan Himself, we can accept them completely without reservation as they are – at least in the beginning. Can't you have at least this much love to understand the difficulty that people sometimes face, the conflict which can last for years, bringing pain and suffering? Should we speak bitterly about them or to them? I don't think so, it is not our true character to do so. We know perhaps that it is not right what others are doing, we know they are going to harm themselves. We know if we give a double-edged razor to our own child that he will cut his fingers. What should we do – throw the child out? Won't a mother with great love say, "Look here, my darling, it is a double-edged razor in your hand and if you are not careful, not vigilant, if you are indifferent, you are going to cut your fingers and they will bleed." The child is completely ignorant. The double-edged razor is something glittering, it attracts his eyes so he holds it in his hands. So why can't we have that same love for the children of God? Love can work miracles, it can heal wound after wound – but it must be pure. In this world an abundance of material things – comforts and luxuries - have been given to us, but we lack love. If love is present then all and everything is present.

It is in love that Bhagavan is saying **prakṛter-guṇa-sammūḍhāḥ** – if they are infatuated, suffering, miserable, then have pity upon them even if they don't want it. Don't say "we have pity on you", but **have** compassion, **have** boundless love in your heart, and then you will see great changes taking place. But let me first start with myself – charity begins at home! We are like them, let us not think that we are superior to them, or they are inferior to us. No! If we have realised the greater half, then we shall have love and compassion as Bhagavan has. Everyone is playing his or her role and let us not poke our nose in anyone's affairs and disturb them. Our duty is to help them and to do that with great, boundless love.

The gifts of nature, of the Divine, are free of cost – the sun, sky, forests – and open to everyone! What does it cost to come here and sit in meditation together, to enjoy mutual happiness? Entrance is absolutely free, anyone can come, just as the river Ganga belongs to everybody. Richness and prosperity are open to all, free of cost. See it, realise it! Don't be lost in the crowd. I am not saying that the crowd is bad, don't misunderstand. Go there also, but go to the bounty of Divine Nature which gives so many lessons that the books cannot give us, and when we realise it our life becomes filled with joy.

What have I given to you? I have only provoked the thoughts and ideas which were already there in you! If you also do the same for your brethren, then this society would be so beautiful to live in, right from this moment. Let us not wait for tomorrow – anything which is good we must start instantly. Everything is provided when you work for that mission. Dedicate your life to that noble cause.

Verse 30

मयि सर्वाणि कर्माणि संन्यस्याध्यात्मचेतसा ।
निराशीर्निर्ममो भूत्वा युध्यस्व विगतज्वरः ॥ ३० ॥

Mayi sarvāṇi karmāṇi sannyasyādhyātma-cetasā I
nirāśīr-nirmamo bhūtvā yudhyasva vigata-jvaraḥ II 30 II

Resigning all thy works to me, with thy consciousness fixed in the Self, being free from desire and egoism, fight, delivered from thy fever.

mayi – in me, the omniscient supreme Lord, the Self of All; sarvāṇi – all; karmāṇi – actions, deeds; sannyasya – renouncing, by dedicating, giving up completely; adhyātma-cetasā – with the mind centred on the Self; nirāśiḥ – free from hope, nirmamaḥ – free from ownership, devoid of egoism; bhūtvā – having become; yudhyasva – fight, engage in battle; vigata-jvaraḥ – free from (mental) fever, i.e. being free from repentance, without remorse.

In the scheme of creation everything in nature is working. A flower is working, and not only for itself, but for the whole of creation, offering itself quietly to something which is not seen with our external eyes. Trees work hard producing fruits and they do not eat their own fruits. There is a law of nature which obliges them to work, and work incessantly and offer their fruits for the whole creation. Fields produce corn, grain, pulses and grass – offering these, not eating it themselves. Walnut, coconut, plantain trees are thought of by us, perhaps, as unintelligent, unconscious, not sensible. It is perhaps that *we* are not sensible, we do not have their keen sense of observation. If we did, then we would see that there is a silent principle which is hard at work to produce, to create, for Her children, all of us. Producing and offering and then renouncing. For what? For the Divine who lives in all of us, for the Self – call it by any name – for the common bondage, the common thread that binds us together. It is for that common thread, that common principle, that this whole creation, the whole of nature is at work.

When we are not reaching out, when we are indifferent to this law, then we begin to work for our petty little selves, to satisfy our little egos, for **my** body, for **my** mind, for **my** feelings, for **my** senses, for **my** appetite. Meeting these needs are also part of the work, but then, if it is isolated from others life would not be possible. There is a kind of link existing between all beings, and this thread has been seen by great seers. They saw that thread (that's why they are called seers), and usually our eyes do not see that invisible thread. When we look at a rosary **(mala)** we see the beads but we forget to see the thread that binds them together. It is with keen eyes that the seers saw the thread on which the pearls were strung, were interwoven together, living together, forming a rosary, a necklace, a garland of flowers. All beings are beautiful garlands of the Divine. We do not know, or we forget, or we are just not conscious, and so we begin to think that "I am all in all". But it is not so, it is also not possible. We have our own individuality, and there are differences – that is the beauty of it. Even on the same tree all the many flowers are similar but no two flowers are identical. No human beings are identical, there are always some differences. No two fruits are identical, and although similar, the differences are there.

You can take individual differences into consideration – call it individuality or personality, but apart from that individualistic way of living, if that common life is forgotten then the individual becomes egoistic and selfish, and may begin to encroach upon the liberty of others. Every flower is an individual. Even on a tree full of flowers, there *is* a place for each flower to express, to grow, to blossom. Their blossoming, their evolution, is not marred because in the scheme of creation there is a place for each flower, for each petal even. Each petal has an accomplishment, is perfect. All parts of a tree have a specific function – the whole tree is as if working to produce a flower. The flower we see, but we do not see it completely because we do not see it with awareness, Pure Self-awareness. Self-awareness does not mean only awareness of my body, eyes and ears – that too is very great. But not only my thoughts, what is happening in the thought of my neighbour sitting next to me is also Self-awareness! Self is so extensive that it lives in my neighbour, the same Self, and I can see very clearly what is happening in his or her mind and heart. Parents know what is happening in the heart of their child, the same with lover and beloved. How can they love if they do not know what is happening in the heart and mind of each other! It is very important in order to have smooth relations.

If we do not know, if our lives are too fast and hectic and we brush aside the illusions, it has disastrous consequences. It can spoil the lives of couples, of individuals, and life becomes restless, unhappy and sad. Then they escape, they don't face each other. First we must face our own Self, and it requires great courage to do so. When you are incapable of facing yourself because you are disturbed, never mind – that happens to all of us! All that is required is to sit quietly, don't speak to anyone, don't complain, don't explain. There are four corners in a room and you can have a corner to yourself. The moment you sit in your corner the disturbance will begin to vaporise like a volatile liquid. But at the time of the disturbance, one forgets that Self-consciousness – Self-awareness, is not there. So those who are sharp, be aware of the Pure Self, because it is only Pure Self which can dissolve the difficulties and problems. For example, if people become angry and speak ill of each other, despise and dislike each other, the problem will not be resolved between them. It will become more complicated. But immediately you sit quietly, Pure Self-awareness descends and at once the problems are solved.

It does not take a long time, but it is strange that we do not know! We have become so extroverted, occupied and engaged in the external world and activities, that sometimes we cease to be introverted. Of course, there must be an equilibrium between the two, our life must be equipoised. There must be a golden mean between introversion and extroversion. It is finally a continuous whole, what is inside is also outside, and what is outside is also inside. But we do not know that – We just think that what is inside my body is "me and mine" and anything that is out of my body is "thou and thine". This "me and mine" and "thou and thine" is a great problem. We have imagined it – in fact the things we "own" were once lying in shops until bought or brought to us, but as soon as we start using and caring for them the sense of possession becomes strong. Can I say that this house belongs to me because I have lived in it for a few years? It doesn't belong to me, it belongs to all who come here. But when there is a "me and mine" and "thou and thine", conflict comes. What are we to do? It is not the teaching of Bhagavan to offend, dislike, suspect, another human being because they behave inconsiderately. Let us be kind, let us be polite and generous. If he or she cannot be generous, then we can be so in our approach, otherwise what is the difference between an ordinary person and we who are living, or pretending to live, the spiritual life? That life must reflect in our behaviour and in the small details of life.

Mahatma Gandhi used to say that anyone can be great on certain great occasions but in the **small** details, in our different walks of life, if we are noble, then that is greatness. Then we give an education to ourselves, an education that may not be given to us in college or university. There, we study for diplomas in order to work in society, and afterwards we have to live and have dealings with people, and these small details occur daily. I do not study the **Bhagavad Gita** for only one hour every day with you, but when I get up early in the morning I reflect upon what I studied, how it shows in my life and mind and behaviour. Was I nice, kind to the people who are coming from outside, or was I only nice to my kith and kin, to my ties, my bondages and bindings, like ordinary families? A stranger, a newcomer from outside, comes, and we should be kind and polite, and we are, if Reality has dawned upon us, if Divine Life has come to us in the real sense of the term. We do not know the newcomer, and we do not know what difficulties he or she is facing. We should be ready from inside to receive that person in the way a mother receives her child who comes in from outside with clothes and body dirty from playing with his friends. She has love for her child and she does not throw him out. She just asks him to wash, or she does it for him. The mother sees her own face as she washes the face of her child and she is loving, kind and affectionate. So it should be natural for us to be kind and generous even to a stranger.

By saying **mayi sarvāṇi karmāṇi sannyasya** – offer all actions to me - Sri Krishna means to the "I" who lives in all. He is identifying with the Supreme Reality. His identification is **not** with his body, mind, feelings and sentiments. We have to understand everything very carefully because each word of the **Bhagavad Gita** is pregnant with meaning, otherwise we would completely misunderstand and might think that Bhagavan is proud of Himself, is selfish, that we should do everything for Him. No! In all your actions He is saying have that spirit, that attitude, of offering all to me. **Sannyasya** means having renounced. Renunciation of what? Renunciation of the fruit of action – it is the fruit, not the action that must be renounced. You can't renounce actions, otherwise life would be impossible, we would not be able to walk, eat, wash or do anything on our own.

You see, Sanskrit was the language of wise people. It is not a dead language, it is the language of dead people! That means usually saints and sages. They become dead to the world in a certain sense – they become quiet, sober. In fact, before they renounce the world they are declared dead! Here in India a ceremony takes place when a person takes **sannyasa** and it is exactly the same ceremony that is performed for a dead person. In life there is so much suffering, sometimes one wants to die to the past. So, in order to have a kind of understanding psychologically of this, a name changing ceremony is performed. We have all suffered. It has been nicely said that we are twice born – once from out of the mother's womb, and the second birth is when we are born in the spiritual life, the Divine Life, the life of Self-enlightenment. It is the second life! It is of that life that Bhagavan Sri Krishna teaches.

Verse 31

ये मे मतमिदं नित्यमनुतिष्ठन्ति मानवाः।
श्रद्धावन्तोऽनसूयन्तो मुच्यन्ते तेऽपि कर्मभिः॥ ३१॥

Ye me matam-idaṁ nityam-anutiṣṭhanti mānavāḥ I
śraddhāvanto'nasūyanto mucyante te'pi karmabhiḥ II 31 II

Those men, too, who, full of faith and free from cavil, constantly follow this teaching of Mine, are released from (the bondage of) works.

ye – those who; me – my; matam – teaching, injunctions; idam – this; nityam – constantly, as an eternal function; anutiṣṭhanti – practice, follow accordingly; mānavāḥ – men, human beings; śraddhāvantaḥ – full of faith and devotion; anasūyantaḥ – not cavilling, without detracting me, without envy; mucyante – are freed; te – they; api – also; karmabhiḥ – from actions.

Matam in Sanskrit means opinion, and in the preceding verses Bhagavan Sri Krishna has expressed His opinion, ideas and attitude towards life. That attitude is an inward one, an attitude of selfless actions so that the Divine transformation takes place in the life of an individual. **Ye me matam-idaṁ nityam** – those who follow my opinion, and this opinion is eternal He says. It is not temporary, it is for all time to come, and it is practicable in all circumstances and walks of life. The condition is that there must be **shraddha**, which means belief plus love and devotion. Wherever there is love there is faith. Doubt comes when love is lacking.

In love we follow because it pleases us, we want to go with, listen to, talk to, the one we love. It is a very natural response and we do it unconsciously even, in our day-to-day life. For the one whom we love we do things effortlessly, it is the flow of our life incessantly. If we do not love we would cease to grow. In faith love is there, and in love actions are performed spontaneously, we cannot do otherwise and then work is really worship and devotion, and all activity is adoration. That is why this approach of action is in devotion, is in love. Somehow or another in love we want to cling. If we find a fragrance of love anywhere we want to stop and smell it, feel and taste it because it gives us pleasure, peace and harmony, and our conflicts are resolved and dissolved.

Trees bear fruits, rivers flow – the unseen love is there, we don't see the love, we see only the expression of it. If someone asks, "how do you love me?", can you show the love? I cannot show any proof of it, yet it is felt. You cannot doubt the existence of the sun. When it shines you can see everything very distinctly, that which was covered by the darkness of night becomes clear in broad daylight. In the same way, during the broad daylight of love, all our actions, activities, movements, all and everything becomes clear. Our life becomes meaningful as soon as we discover love in our life, it becomes purposeful and has a direction. Otherwise, our life without love becomes like a rudderless boat moving aimlessly in the water.

For Bhagavan, of course love is unconditional, completely pure and selfless, devoid of any motives – you just love because you feel it. There is no expectation. And it is in such a love that everything in our life becomes absolutely clear, otherwise our ideas are clouded and our minds confused because this kind of love has not dawned upon us. Just as soon as the lamp burns the fund of oil finds the purpose. As soon as the lamp is kindled the whole oil is transformed into light and then everything becomes clear. It is the same when the lamp of love is burned in our life for whoever, even in the world. Love in the world is not meaningless. It had been given to us so we can realise the taste, the fruits, the rewards. The reward of love is instantaneous – that is the beauty of love. That's why we do not expect the reward, the fruits of love, because joy and happiness – the return – is immediate. In the world, when you work, you get the return in the evening, or after a month, in the form of a wage. But in love it is not so, it is instantaneous as soon as you love. Even with the idea of love the heart quickens; there is something quite magical about love. Without love society would be like a desert land. It is the greenery of love which makes this world beautiful.

So, when this love is intertwined with belief it is called **shraddha**. We have **shraddha** for example for our Master – for Bhagavan, for our parents and to those who are superior in virtues because in their presence our life becomes secured. Everybody is seeking for security in life and when there is security then one expresses, opens and blossoms, like a bud into a flower. That is our real tendency, the natural course of our heart and life from within. You cannot create **shraddha** in anyone, you cannot impose it on anybody. **Shradhha** comes from within, one feels and one offers. When it comes you cannot do otherwise. It is only the one who understands the value of these deeper feelings who begins to have some kind of **shradhha**. Bhagavan is like this. He understands the feelings, devotion and sentiments of His devotees and that is why they have faith in Him, **shradhha**.

Bhagavan is saying in this verse that the opinion He has expressed to Arjuna is not temporary, here today and tomorrow not. To His devotee He is saying, "I am incapable of changing My opinion, it is unchangeable. I can't change it in spite of Myself." **Ye me matam-idaṁ nityam – nityam** means eternal – this opinion will last forever. Many opinions that we express in our life have temporary existence. They hold good for today and tomorrow they change. But Bhagavan says to Arjuna, "Work in love and work in devotion, devoid of expectation of the fruits of action; this is my opinion and it is eternal."

Please understand this, realise it and experience it. The sooner you realise it the better it is and you will be unburdened in your life of the great shackles of activity. Everybody is bound by these shackles, by the bondage of activity. See how people are working; at first they like it but afterwards the work becomes very difficult. It becomes a drudgery and they do not want to work and yet there is no alternative. Bhagavan is showing us an alternative, a way out which is possible and feasible. Where is the impossibility in it? Where is the difficulty in what Bhagavan is expressing? Is it in working for the sake of love? In love, when you work, it is no more a burden, so where is the difficulty! Working for money, working with the expectation of something in return, very often brings frustration, disappointment and disillusionment. We are running after illusions and not finding the way out of the vicious circle that life has become. It is so difficult to come out of it. Easy to talk about it but not easy to come out of it. Bhagavan is showing the way out, but you have to touch the circle, you have to put your finger somewhere on the circle, and that is a beginning. Bhagavan says this is His eternal opinion – work, but work for the sake of love.

The word **manavah** is full of significance. It means the descendent of **Manu**. Manu is the most primordial man, and also means the great thinker and philosopher Manu, whose work on the constitution of social life is widely read in India. So the descendants of **Manu**, thinking beings, full of faith and devotion, perform their activities not as an obligation, not as an imposition.

Śhraddhāvantonasūyantaḥ – ana means "not", and **asuyā** means "envy". What is this envy, why do we become envious in this life? I think our response of envy comes from a lack of something within our own self and when we see someone having in abundance what we lack, we become envious. With envy we can come to despise or hate another and a blockage results. In love there is communication. Bhagavan is a great soul and could be envied. If someone is devotional and loving, then all the virtues of Bhagavan shall be transferred to him or her, free of cost, a pure gift. But in envy, the virtues will not come, they cannot be transferred. The energy is the same – hate and love – but one is expressed in a negative way and the other in a positive way. It is much better to love than to be envious, and again it is much better to love than to be jealous. Jealousy is that mixed up, painful, disagreeable feeling that comes to all of us at times. If somehow our love is great and we can make some sacrifice (which is not easy) then jealousy will not appear.

Jealousy consumes energy and is a waste of energy, a distortion. We become frustrated, we are losers – we do not gain anything by being jealous. We are advised to transcend it, which is not easy to do because when we become victims of jealousy, are seized by it, then we are completely enveloped in it. It is harmful for the one who is jealous and for the one towards whom the jealousy is directed because love is not free to express itself. In love you grow, you outgrow, you transcend, but in jealousy you are blocked, the mind is blocked. We don't like to be jealous, and yet we are. We do not like the disagreeable feeling it brings. It is an obstacle in spiritual life – that is why Bhagavan is saying not to become envious. It is a hurdle placed in our way, and if our love is strong we shall outgrow and overcome the hurdle. So, Bhagavan is asking us to transcend this envious state of mind from within ourselves, to overcome this discontented, resentful, disagreeable attitude towards another. **Mucyante tepi karmabhiḥ** – those who are not envious transcend the shackles, the bondage of actions.

In what a great psychological, detailed, vivid way these things have been analysed! In love all is possible. When we absorb and imbibe these teachings in our own lives they are really an act of devotion.

Verse 32

ये त्वेतदभ्यसूयन्तो नानुतिष्ठन्ति मे मतम्।
सर्वज्ञानविमूढांस्तान्विद्धि नष्टानचेतसः॥ ३२॥

Ye tvetad-abhyasūyanto nānutiṣṭhanti me matam I
sarvajñāna-vimūḍhāṁstān-viddhi naṣṭān-acetasaḥ II 32 II

But those who slight my teaching and do not follow it, know them to be blind to all wisdom, lost and senseless.

ye – those who; tu – but, however; etat – this instruction of Mine; abhyasūyantaḥ – carping at, decrying, out of envy; na – not; anutiṣṭhanti – practise, follow, regularly perform; me – my; matam – teaching; sarvajñāna-vimūḍhān – deluded in all knowledge; tān – them; viddhi – know; naṣṭān – ruined; acetasaḥ – devoid of discrimination.

Again **tu** indicates that Bhagavan Sri Krishna's thinking is taking a turn. Whereas before He had been speaking of those who follow the divine law, in this verse He is referring to those who do not. There is a divine law which binds us all together, in fact it binds the entire universe. If we do not face it, if we try to escape it, we suffer. When we observe it we are completely in peace and harmony – completely in correspondence with each other everywhere, in all walks of life. When we sit here in meditation it is to become aware of that divine law, and observe our thinking process. At least for a short time we can be introverted, most of the time we are turned outward – which is also part of our life. We cannot always be in meditation. If by meditation we mean to close the eyes, sit in darkness, or do nothing, then such would not be possible throughout the day – if indeed this is what meditation means. The meditation that we perform here, for a short time, we call Divine Meditation; so called because it gives us divine consciousness. We become aware about the divine law which is already in all of us in the form of the Self.

Everybody is moving, thinking, speaking and conducting themselves in accordance with the Self and sometimes one is aware and sometimes one is not aware. When we sit together in meditation we join the collective Self. Individual tendencies are there according to individual needs – we move, work, act – that is part of our life. Everybody needs a moment of silence; sometimes we are aware of the need and sometimes not. As soon as you begin to follow this divine law of meditation then you are in harmony. What would be our life if we were not able to sit in peace and silence even for a moment! We live as a small family, the problems of others are ours – in fact there are no others because in them our Self is also living. Nobody in this world can live alone. If independence means to live according to personal whims, not thinking of others, then that is selfish and that we are not supposed to be. Everybody of course, more or less, is selfish but at the same time our Self lives in others, and there are people who are working for us to provide food, shelter and clothing. Thus, in return we have to do something. Outside in society there is restlessness. People are very active but if there is love between us then work is a joy. It is this principle which Bhagavan has laid down in previous verses and especially in this one.

Now, in contrast, He is giving the example of a person who is contemptuous of the divine law and does not respect it. To disrespect divine law would be to disrespect one's own Self! It is this divine law which Krishna brings to our attention, awareness, so that our minds are no more narrow and do not think of our own petty little self. Ego is the cause of all problems and it is difficult to get rid of this ego. But, if we want a harmonious life we have to sacrifice this petty ego and think in broader terms. Whatever knowledge we possess, all of it is meaningless in the absence of awareness of this divine principle, this divine love. Bhagavan feels uncomfortable about such people who do not have the consciousness of common good, who do not think about the welfare of all. Those who do think of the welfare of all are truly noble people: "Blessed are the poor in spirit for they shall see God; blessed are the peacemakers for they shall be called the children of God." These sayings of Jesus are not religious teachings. We should try to live them in our lives. It is about the same divine principles that Bhagavan Sri Krishna is speaking and He is stating that those who are not aware of the divine principle which enables us to live, to coexist harmoniously in this world, are blind.

You see, there are apparently differences of many kinds – language, culture, faith – and yet behind the differences is a unity in diversity. It is difficult to discover that unity. The diversities are obvious from outside but the unity is seen from within, and that is only possible when hearts and minds are probed and we become aware of that common bond, thread, that exists in all of us. Bhagavan is making us aware of that common good, common welfare, laid down in the **Yamas** and **Niyamas**. Divine Meditation will not be possible unless and until we observe these rules in our lives. Our minds must be cleansed – a very difficult task. **Manas** (mind), intellect and ego are the three constituent parts of our **antahkarana** – (**antah** means internal, and **karana** means sense organ). We are trying to analyse and study our thought processes – **manas** – as we sit in meditation. Superior to that is intellect – **buddhi** –

the sense of discrimination. **Buddhi** actually means the awakening inside. When we awaken to the Divine Reality it is with the help of the intellect. So this **buddhi**, when it is awakened to the Divine Reality, is not only a storehouse of thoughts and knowledge but also awakening to discrimination – the sense of what is right and what is wrong. It is not my task to tell you that; you have to discover for yourself. If I tell you, you may accept it out of love and obligation but it will not convince you. When it comes entirely from yourself, when you begin to feel its urge, when you have enough of life and suffering, then you come to the conclusion that there are certain things which must be followed and other things have to be given up, by **yourself.** And that is the dawning of the sense of wisdom, and that is the task of the **buddhi.** In that awakening there is no anger, hatred or jealousy.

There is no selfishness at all, no darkness or ignorance -no ego. Self is always enlightened but we are not aware of it, rather like a lamp with a glass cover. Sometimes the glass becomes black due to smoke from the burning oil. In the same way, our flame is burning incessantly – if it were not we simply could not exist. So the flame is there and sometimes smoke is also present and we are not capable of seeing the flame because of hatred, jealousy and anger. So we sit, we think, reflect upon and try to remove that lamp black, the smoke that has accumulated on the glass, and as soon as it is removed the glass is again transparent and you can see the flame. And there is no gust of wind so the flame does not flicker, it is steady. We need air otherwise the flame will not burn, but we do not want gusts of wind like the temptations of life – those illusions after which we are running madly. As we come to the evening of our lives we begin to realize that that is what we have been doing.

As soon as that consciousness dawns upon us it means that we have purified our **antahkarana**.

Before there is Self-awareness **sadhana** must be done for self-purification. Self-enlightenment is not like a magic lamp, a will-of-the-wisp. It will not just come! We have to work for it and that is what we are trying to do. We must do **sadhana** and we learn it from our masters. People sometimes try to do it with drugs and when the effects wear off the mind is just the same as before, and addictions can result. Meditation is not an addiction. It is the most divine, natural process. Peace is the urge of the soul. Everybody wants peace, not restlessness, not disturbance, not hatred. Everybody likes sweet words, loving words and politeness. Out of this wisdom, this divine knowledge, all our good manners have come.

All that we want for you is that you become peaceful and harmonious. This society will be worthwhile when we begin to think of others. We all are living for a certain purpose and without that aim our life is like a rudderless boat moving in a circle – we cannot advance. And that is what is happening in society – there is a great whirlpool that people are seized by and there is no way out. And it is this that **Vedanta** calls **maya**. **Maya** is not something which you can see with the outward eyes but it is this: that we do not know why we are earning, we do not know why we are eating, sleeping, building, etc. Life has not been given to us to live thoughtlessly. At least once in our life we must face ourselves howsoever difficult it may be! But people lack the courage to do so, they are not ready for a self-operation. A surgeon can operate on others but not on himself. In this spiritual life there is no other way except to operate on our own self, to be our own surgeon. I cannot do it for you. I can suggest something and it may be painful for you, but it is just advice from outside. Self-realization is a self-operation! Try to understand the magnitude of Self-realization. It does not come overnight, it is not like an Aladdin's lamp. For Self-realization you have to have patience and perseverance, and be ardent in your desire for it. Your Self-study **(svadhyaya)** must be intense, and the **Bhagavad Gita**, the **Upanishads** and the **Brahmasutras** are the three texts which are an aid to Self-study.

Verse 33

सदृशं चेष्टते स्वस्याः प्रकृतेर्ज्ञानवानपि ।
प्रकृतिं यान्ति भूतानि निग्रहः किं करिष्यति ॥ ३३ ॥

Sadṛśaṁ ceṣṭate svasyāḥ prakṛter-jñānavān-api I
prakṛtiṁ yānti bhūtāni nigrahaḥ kiṁ kariṣyati II 33 II

Even the man of knowledge acts in accordance with his own nature. Beings follow their nature. What can repression accomplish.

sadṛśam – in accordance; ceṣṭate – acts, behaves; svasyāḥ – of his own; prakṛteḥ – modes of nature; jñānavān – a wise man, a man of wisdom; api – even, although; prakṛtim – to nature; yānti – follow, undergo; bhūtāni – beings, all living entities; nigrahaḥ – restraint, repression; kim – what; kariṣyati – will do.

The man of knowledge means a person who has studied only the scriptures but is not Self-enlightened. His wisdom is confined to the scriptures. You have knowledge about India before you come but you are devoid of experience until you arrive and see people face to face. That is direct experience and that only comes when you are going to that country; only then you have become Realized. Indeed, there is place for our **sadhana** and studying the scriptures, because some kind of improvement takes place. We cannot say that it is useless – it is useful, but it is relative. It is still not absolute until one is enlightened. Imperfections and weaknesses are there, differences too, otherwise there would be no place for wisdom and people would cease to make an effort. It would be of no use to study the Scriptures. At least in them you have the intellectual, the verbal knowledge. There are some people not even aware of them – just engrossed in their lives and suffering. They do not know a way out but are just caught in a vicious circle. They want to come out of it but cannot – they are helpless.

We are all at some time in such circumstances, in such a vicious circle. We do not know where to come out of it, we want to jump out but the centrifugal force is so strong that again and again we are rejected and so remain in that circle. We become a victim of it and consequently suffer, and we simply do not know what to do. Then we make one last effort, and there is help from outside, and it helps us to transcend the condition. It is as if you leave Earth. Your body is affected by gravitational force to some certain extent, then, as you see in pictures from space stations, everything floats freely. Such an experience also comes when you meditate. You float and feel that you are leaving, but then the pull of the rocket is there and you come back again to the Earth. Even if you go to another planet the pull is present. Those people who live in the transcendental region have transcended the effects of all planets, they are not subjected to any influence. They are the chosen few – Krishna, Rama, Buddha, Christ – they willed it and made the way. Divine Grace was there – Divine Grace is always present, but they utilised it and with its help they went beyond.

We sit here together for mutual understanding and to understand what we are studying, which is the **Bhagavad Gita**. It helps us to unfold ourselves, to realize our Self, to enable us to have Self-awareness, Self-consciousness. We are in the chain of actions and reactions, taken up in that vicious circle. Why?

The mental sheath consists of **sancita karma** which means collective or stored actions done in the previous life, and **prarabdha karma** which means actions we have sown in the form of a seed and which are now sprouting, and in sprouting they must grow. That action, seed, has to become a plant, a tree and bear fruit. For **sancita karmas,** stored in seed form and which have not been sown as yet, naturally the sprout is not there. If Self-enlightenment has come (it also depends on its frequency, strength and intensity) and if it is acute and sharp, then those seeds of **sancita karma** not yet sown are roasted, so to speak, and roasted seeds can not sprout. Name and form are there but the inner potential has disappeared, so having no potential to sprout and grow they cannot bear fruit. For **prarabdha karmas**, the seeds of action already sown and sprouting and they **must** complete the course (until and unless **brahmanistha,** which is a very high state of consciousness, is attained – in that state **prarabdha karmas** also disappear). So for the Self-enlightened person those seeds of action which have already been set in motion and have attained momentum will not stop. Just like an arrow from a bow – it has to go right up to the target – it is difficult to stop it between the bow and target. The great saints and sages were of the opinion that **prarabdha karmas** were difficult to stop.

The third kind of action is called **kriyamana karma** which are the actions we are still going to do. Even a Self-enlightened person will not be able to do without activities. In verse five of this chapter Bhagavan said, "**Na hi kascit kṣaṇam api**" – Not even for a moment can a person live without doing activity, it is the function of nature, it *has* to be done. Even when you come here and sit in meditation your mind is functioning and if you are vigilant about your process of thinking you will see how many thoughts of past experience come. All kinds of memories come, sometimes sweet, sometimes bitter or happy or sad, and you see that the mind is active. Even in the dream state of consciousness the individual is working.

Often I say to you that it is so painful to free oneself. It is a great suffering but when you are doing something sincerely with understanding, in light, there is a reward. Peace, serenity, joy, happiness, wisdom come. Light comes – your face shines, your eyes are full of light and people see it. From outside who will not see a kindled light? – even a small child knows when a lamp is kindled. Why make such an effort? If only past actions have to bear fruit then where is the place for our effort, for our **sadhana**? We would not be optimistic about **sadhana** and pessimism would surround us. But after repeated pessimistic moments, optimism comes and you do not accept any defeat. You go on fighting because then there is the energy – call it by any name – which takes you a step forward.

I am talking to you and this action is being stored and it is preparing the future actions. You, too, are creating your own destiny by sitting here, as you also would have, had you chosen to be somewhere else. The law of action is inflexible, immutable and so scientific. And it is about this law of action that Bhagavan has been describing in this third chapter. It doesn't refer to an ordinary activity like that of a labourer – that too is included – but to this action of sitting here reflecting, meditating. It is creating your future. Really, I tell you how very fortunate we are to be here, engrossed in something very creative and substantial. We are preparing the **prarabdha karma**! Buddha emphasised to his followers that if they think rightly they will speak rightly and act rightly. Right thinking is that thinking which never comes in conflict with anyone. You will ask if there is such thinking? Yes, provided that such thinking is in consonance with Self-enlightenment because it is the Self and Self alone that lives in all, and in right thinking Self-awareness begins to dawn on us. A Self-enlightened person does not only think of the majority or the minority, he thinks for all.

The great Upanishadic thinkers said, '**Sarve bhavantu sukhinaḥ**, which means "let all be happy". **All** without exception, because they knew that in all is the same Self, the same Divine Being. And they knew that to be in opposition or conflict is not good. They found out a way of living in India for the welfare of all. Just as the rising of the sun is in the interests of all, in the same way Self-enlightenment is in the interests of all. When you work while you are in Self-awareness it is not selfish awareness because selfishness is a diminutive term of Self while Self-awareness is a term independent in itself. A Self-aware person sees all that is in himself, and all that is in the objective world, like a kindled lamp. So it is in this consciousness the great **Rishis** were absorbed. When we meditate we try to become aware, to be established in the Self, in the Divine which is continuously flowing from us but we are simply not aware. We have to purify the mind, intellect and ego.

You think that you are a small thing. No! You are involved with the entire world, universe, cosmos! It depends upon how much you are aware of your Pure Self and to what degree. Usually people are narrow-minded just like a frog in a well. Their notions are very limited and with this they are very satisfied to spend their lives, finish and go away! Some people are not like this. Buddha, Krishna and Christ are souls who were not satisfied with a narrow sheepish outlook. They expanded, they radiated like the sun's rays. It is only in love and devotion Reality unveils Itself. You can't force it. Prayer is not a force, yet it is the force of all forces, it has great potency. The great seers living in the forests chanted divine mantras and **sutras** such as **Hiraṇmayena pātreṇa satyasyāpihitaṁ mukhaṁ tat-tvaṁ pūṣnnapāvṛṇu satyadharmāya dṛṣṭaye**, which means "the face of Truth is covered with a golden disc. Remove it, O Pushan, so that I, who love the Truth, may see it." Pushan is a name for the sun. Such is the prayer which comes to us only when we transcend the limit of **prakriti**. That means the mind (**manas**), the intellect (**buddhi**), and the ego (**ahankara**). All merge into the Divine Self. Unless and until the call comes from within, the way out of the vicious circle will not be found.

Verse 34

इन्द्रियस्येन्द्रियस्यार्थे रागद्वेषौ व्यवस्थितौ ।
तयोर्न वशमागच्छेत्तौ ह्यस्य परिपन्थिनौ ॥ ३४ ॥

Indriyasyendriyasyārthe rāgadveṣau vyavasthitau I
tayor-na vaśam-āgacchet-tau hy-asya paripanthinau II 34 II

Senses have attachment and aversion to their respective objects; none should be swayed by them. They are indeed obstacles in man's path.

Indriyasya – of the senses, of all the organs; indriyasya-arthe – in the object of the senses; rāgadveṣau – attachment and aversion, attraction and repulsion; vyavasthitau – seated, ordained by nature, are sure to occur; tayoḥ – of these two; na – not; vaśam – sway; āgacchet – should come under; tau – these two; hi – verily; asya – his; paripanthinau – foes.

As long as we are bound by **prakriti** (nature) hatred, anger and jealousy will come to us because it is nature which is at work. An ordinary person is under the command of **prakriti** but a person who has transcended it comes to a state of Pure Self-awareness. He is no more a slave, he is a master of his own destiny. He has come out of the circumference of **prakriti** and arrived at the state of Self-realisation where there is no aversion or attachment. On the plane of the senses there is attachment, aversion, hatred, anger and jealousy. In the previous verse Bhagavan Sri Krishna said very clearly that everybody, except the wise who have knowledge of the Self, is subjected to **prakriti**. We experience attraction towards desirable things (**raga**) and repulsion towards undesirable things (**dvesha**). In each object of our sense perceptions there is attachment, attraction, or aversion, repulsion. Both these are said to be like two robbers who rob the individual on the pilgrimage to liberation.

In attraction there is an action, and in aversion there is a reaction – to every action there is an equal and opposite reaction. So, attraction and aversion are the two extremes of the same reality. The one who is attracted is also repulsed – the actions are different. Both are established. In experiencing an object which you like there is an attachment. Bhagavan Patanjali says in one of his **sutras: Sukhānuśayī rāgaḥ** (2:7) and **dukhānuśayī dvesaḥ** (2:8) – pleasure leads to desire and emotional attachment, and unhappiness leads to hatred. To that which gives us pleasure we get attached, and in pain, sorrow and unhappiness sleeps the child of aversion. It means that where there is pain there is aversion; it is a natural process. Pleasure generates greed and lust which strengthens attachment and stimulates a greater craving and one wants more and more. Unfulfilled desires lead to sorrow. In extreme distress man comes to hate himself, his family, neighbours and surroundings.

The sages often gave the following example to show how the mind appears to take on the colour of what attaches or repulses us: when **japa kusuma**, a red flower, is placed beside a quartz, the quartz takes on the beautiful scarlet colour of the flower, but reverts back to its transparent, translucent beauty when the **japa kusuma** is removed. The jewel is impermeable so colour does not penetrate. And this is the case of the mind when the consciousness gets attached. That is why attachment, attraction, aversion, diversion and divergence are not the solution of the problem. Then what can be done?

Everywhere in the world we see the consequences of attachment or detachment, repulsion or aversion which are creating this drama of life. If attachment and aversion were not at the root of our conduct and behaviour life would be peaceful. For example, in meditation there is neither attachment or aversion. In this pure meditation all problems are resolved. Bhagavan Sri Krishna says that the real state of meditation is neither obtained in attachment or detachment nor attained in attraction or repulsion or aversion. In both cases the individual is not in the state of equanimity, of equilibrium. In real pure and divine love, in Pure Self-awareness, you are neither in attraction nor in repulsion; there is just a state of being.

Our goal is to evolve into the Divine. Senses are stumbling blocks to it. We have to transcend them – it is from attachment and aversion they get the power to function. When these dualities are slowly disappearing the senses cease to be enemies. Love and hatred, likings or dislikings are created by the egoistic attitude. At times families cannot bear to be together even for one hour. Just as there was a spark of attraction there is a spark of aversion and they want to split, to separate. If a sense of wisdom dawns upon us then where is the need to go to the courts to settle disputes? Conflicts are very intricate – as we face them in life they can become unbearable. We want a solution and so we run from ashram to ashram thinking to find a saintly monk, a **siddha purusa**, to solve our difficulties. We do this with great faith and aspirations and when the desire is not fulfilled we are frustrated and disappointed. We do not know that where the problem arises, there **also** is the solution. Like the story of the old lady who was searching for a needle under a lamppost. A passer-by asks, "Where did you lose the needle?" "In my room," replies the old lady. "Then why don't you look for it in your room?" says the passer-by. "Because," says the old lady, "there is no light in my room!"

That is what most of us are doing – we are seeking the needle of knowledge and wisdom outside of ourselves. People are confused, restless, disturbed, and do not know that it is only by becoming Self-aware that problems and conflicts are resolved. And that is difficult – no one is ready to face the Self because it is so painful to do.

Desire for worldly things must be converted into the desire for God. The teachings of the scriptures, of the **Bhagavad Gita**, exhort us to change our attitude from the base to the noble. When life for the individual is converted into the life of God the senses cease to be enemies. Courage and perseverance will take us to the goal, attachment and aversion will not.

Verse 35

श्रेयान्स्वधर्मो विगुणः परधर्मात्स्वनुष्ठितात् ।
स्वधर्मे निधनं श्रेयः परधर्मो भयावहः ॥ ३५ ॥

Śreyān-svadharmo viguṇaḥ paradharmāt-svanuṣṭhitāt I
svadharme nidhanaṁ śreyaḥ paradharmo bhayāvahaḥ II 35 II

Better is one's law though imperfectly carried out than the law of another carried out perfectly. Better is death in (the fulfilment of) one's own law, for to follow another's law is perilous.

Śreyān – far better, superior to; svadharmaḥ – one's own duty; vigunaḥ – devoid of merit, defective, deficient; paradharmāt – than the duty of another; svanuṣṭhitāt – than well discharged, well performed; svadharme – in one's own duty; nidhanam – death, destruction; śreyaḥ – better; paradharmaḥ – another's duty; bhayāvahaḥ – fraught with fear.

For a **sadhaka** it is important to know one's own nature and to work on it. That is what we are doing when we meditate. We are unfolding ourselves – our mind is unfolding; it is relaxing and in this realisation it evolves. The essential nature of yourself takes time to show itself. In meditation you are face to face with yourself and freedom of thinking must be there – you allow thoughts to come and you observe them. Otherwise, how does one know about one's own self? If you proceed according to your own nature, and if you are a keen observer and capable of seeing yourself unfolding, **then** you grow. People are gifted to do different things and they have specific inclinations and interests which come from within. For example, a student comes to know that he is gifted in the subject of history but his father wants him to become a doctor. Obviously the father does not know or understand his son's nature and instead of helping him to develop his gift and to grow, he forces him to become a doctor.

The **Bhagavad Gita** helps us in our daily life. Bhagavan does not speak of anything which is not practicable or which is not feasible. Being a responsible person He speaks of what is in the reach of our own self. Thinking is a very important faculty and many people do not use it – they are biased, or have some kind of incognition, or they are conditioned. Here, we want to be de-conditioned, which is not an easy thing. Very often we are conditioned by some taboos, traditions or religions. I do not deny the importance of all these. Please do not misunderstand, we must take them into consideration as influences upon our thinking which, at the same time, nourish our mind. There are certain habits, manners, ways of living and thinking, ways of feeling which may lead to misunderstanding between individuals and nations.

Like a transplanted tree we, too, face difficulties when we are placed in an entirely new atmosphere. We may face insurmountable problems as we probe into our own nature in this process of growth. All of these things seek expression and it is part of our nature. We are trying to interpret "one's own nature" and think about what Bhagavan means by **svadharma** (one's own law) and **paradharma** (the law of another) in this 35th verse.

Conditioning is something which does not allow us to grow – much like the way the feet of women in China were bound at birth to prevent them from growing because it was considered that small feet were beautiful. Our minds are sometimes conditioned by our beliefs, traditions and religions, which do not allow us to grow. We have to grow!

Human beings get attached to sense objects. When we see something beautiful we want to see it over and over again, and in time we get attached to it. Later on we realise the attachment causes problems. We all experience attachment and aversion and the consequences of both. In the 34th verse Bhagavan made us aware of attachment and aversion and gave a warning to the person who is established in the material world. In the beginning we get attached to all the sensual pleasures of life and then comes an aversion. It is something in nature – we all feel and experience it and we may not be able to explain it. Like a magnet and iron filings; in the beginning the iron filings are attracted to the magnet and afterwards repulsion occurs. We have to be careful and try to find a golden mean between the two extremes so that we take care of the attachment before it is transformed into an aversion – into hatred and dislike.

So we must deal with our nature, this prakriti with its three **gunas** – **sattva** (the quality of harmony), **rajas** (the quality of activity) and **tamas** (the quality of darkness and inertia). If we are to proceed on the path to **sattvaguna** then the elimination of **rajoguna** and **tamoguna** is required. **Tamoguna** is transcended with the help of **rajoguna,** and **rajoguna** is transcended with the help of **sattvaguna**. As we sit here studying the **Bhagavad Gita** we are in **sattvaguna** in which we are in accordance with each other; we are in harmony. These three **gunas** are necessary to some extent, but they have to be transcended for a person to be in the state of Self-awareness.

Up to the 34th verse of chapter three Bhagavan is probing into the mind of a **sadhaka** who is on the path of

Self-realisation and He warns of where there are pitfalls and loopholes. It is not only a path of roses – there are also thorns. All of us experience this path as such – all kinds of mental attitudes, observations and actions come to us. Before they come, Bhagavan warns us not to become the victims of attachment and aversion which are the two extremes. Both are like two highway robbers who deprive the traveller of his possessions; deprive the person on the path of Self-realisation of his spiritual wealth. When attachment and aversion come, spiritual knowledge and virtues can be taken away.

Now in this 35th **sloka** Bhagavan comes to speak about the Self, and that Self-realisation is called **svadharma** which means the law of the Self, or the divine law, or the Kingdom of Heaven. Bhagavan is saying **śreyān-svadharmo viguṇaḥ** – the divine law is superior. In previous verses Bhagavan was describing the material world and He used the term `and now the word he uses for the same **prakriti** is **paradharma**. The Self is closest to us and the material world is **para** and **para** means far away, different – this objective world is far away from the Self. Self is not far – you are Self. So Bhagavan has divided the cosmic world into two laws of life. One is of nature – **prakriti**, the material law and the objective world – and the other is **svadharma** – the divine law. Before people become victims of anger, hatred and jealousy, Bhagavan sends wisdom to dawn upon them and they will see that there is a spiritual law which also governs the world, and that law is higher.

If we do not follow the spiritual path – the law of the Self – the alternative is there. We cannot stay in a vacuum forever. We are either on the path of Self-realisation or we are not. It depends entirely on you. Bhagavan is speaking not to frighten us, He is simply putting the Truth in front of us. Be warned that where there is pleasure there will be pain also, and where there is attachment there will be aversion. How to find the golden mean, the balance, between the two is the task of divine life which Bhagavan calls **svadharma**.

Verse 36

अर्जुन उवाच।
अथ केन प्रयुक्तोऽयं पापं चरति पूरुषः।
अनिच्छन्नपि वार्ष्णेय बलादिव नियोजितः॥ ३६॥

Arjuna uvāca I
Atha kena prayukto'yaṁ pāpaṁ carati pūruṣaḥ I
anicchann-api vārṣṇeya balād-iva niyojitaḥ II 36 II

Arjuna said, Now, impelled by what does man commit sin? O Krishna, *though loath to sin, he is driven to it forcibly, as it were.*

atha – now, then; kena – by which; prayuktaḥ – impelled; ayam – this; pāpaṁ – sin; carati – does, commit; pūruṣaḥ – man; anicchan – not wishing, though not himself wishing; api – even; vārṣṇeya – o scion of the Vṛṣṇi dynasty; balāt – by force; iva – as it were; niyojitaḥ – constrained, engaged.

In this 36th **sloka** how has the idea of sin come to the mind of Arjuna? Has he found the seed of such a question in the statements of Bhagavan Sri Krishna in **slokas** 34 or 35? If a person is established in his senses he will be pulled towards sensuous objects. Some desires, passions and lusts will come to his mind. There will be room, a place in his mind for these **only** when he is not Self-established. Where is the room in the mind of a person who is meditating, or studying sacred scriptures, for anything other than Self? He is left free. That is why in the beginning it is difficult for people to understand this state of meditation and to study noble scriptures which prevent them from following a sinful life, a life of evil. See how people just break the rules – as soon as they are asked to come to **satsang** they say, "No, it doesn't give us liberty." If you cannot rise then you have to fall down – there is no other course left.

So, people who live the life of the senses are easily led into a lustful life and suffer afterwards. Mental problems are the consequence. It is easy to slip, to fall down, but it is difficult to climb. A dead fish can go with the current in a river but it cannot go against the current. It is a living fish which can resist the flow of the current. People are blind – when they become the subject of lust they are not sensible at that time. Afterwards, they feel sad and the vicious circle goes on. People beat each other, quarrel and kill, and sometimes commit suicide. From such things Bhagavan Sri Krishna wants to protect us. Love is the message of the **Bhagavad Gita** but how can blind-folded people see the beauty of it? Those who live a righteous life suffer too, but there is a strength of the soul, which comes only when you live a Self-possessed and disciplined, pure and chaste life. You are fearless! Our path is not easy, it is a path of thorns and those who are afraid of thorns, let them not come! We will not submit to the evils of society and people. We are not fighting against people but we are fighting against evil. We love people. We don't hate the sinner but we certainly hate the sin because the consequence is suffering, sadness, depression and violence. These are the seeds which are found in the two previous verses.

Now Arjuna questions: **atha kena prayuktoyaṁ pāpaṁ carati pūruṣaḥ** – Impelled by what does a man commit sin? Ordinarily a man thinks that it is the woman who tempts a man or seduces him. Truthfully speaking, a woman does not seduce a man and it is only the **Bhagavad Gita** which can say this so fearlessly. Rather it is due to the seed of temptation – hidden lust and desire – in the man. The text of the **Bhagavad Gita** speaks boldly! Some people despise women – for what purpose? When you have realised your Self, when wisdom has dawned upon you, then a woman is no more a woman, she is a goddess, she is a mother, and you can worship her. Shiva worshipped His consort Parvati for her beauty and strength; there was no temptation in her, no passion. When a woman or a man becomes pure, then he or she is worshipped. As long as a man considers a woman an object for the satisfaction of his desires he has not realised her real beauty, and will never be able to love her. That's what is happening in our society worldwide – today two people are in love, tomorrow they are separating. What kind of game is going on – do you want to be a part of this? Yoga is not a few acrobatic exercises, as people think, to have a handsome body, a strong body in order to indulge over and over again in the lust of passion!

Let me tell you that once in the Indian Embassy in Brussels Sri Aurobindo's Centenary was being celebrated. There was a teacher of **Yoga Asanas**, who said: "Aurobindo has not said to observe the **Brahmacharya** (chastity) life – it is not necessary." Then the lion-like person Jean Herbert from France (who had lived with Aurobindo and translated his books) said: "How can you speak like this? How can you perform **yoga asanas** in the absence of **brahmacharya**, which is an essential constituent part of Yoga?" Jean Herbert knew the truth and so he could speak with force. Today hundreds of Yoga teachers are spoiling the masses. You see what such people have done in the name of Yoga – corruption! So, go and improve it, gird your loins and prepare for the Truth of life. Think about it. It is only a powerful person who will be able to digest this message of Truth. The **Rishis** say that it is not by a weak person that the Self can be realised. Observe discipline in your life and try to sacrifice everything for it.

Self-realisation is very subtle, abtruse and noble. It is not easily seizable. In the previous verses Bhagavan was trying to have Arjuna understand this by himself. A real master does not force or oblige the disciple, but prepares the disciple from inside and helps him to realise what he should do. Dictation is not the path of the master. In both master and disciple the same Self is dwelling – the only difference is that one is aware and the other is not aware. The teacher understands what the disciple is experiencing because he, too, was once a disciple. All the great souls have passed through intricate conflicts, otherwise they would not have been able to guide the masses. There is hardly anyone (except perhaps a Self-realised person) who does not have conflict in his or her life. **Guru** in Sanskrit means heavy (not in body weight), i.e. a person possessing the latent force, the potency, of his spiritual life. He understands the subtleties of life, which is why we go before him and even worship him. Highly elevated souls will never like to put themselves on a high pedestal, to have their body worshipped by others. It is the soul that they want people to be aware of and to worship.

So a conflict arises in the mind of Arjuna because he is incapable of finding out what the soul, the Self is. It is very difficult to find this out, and becomes more so as we grow up and pass through the storms of life. As old age comes we begin to think that we are missing something, and when the time of departure comes we are fearful, and attached to possessions. If the one thing we are given to do (which is to realise the Self) had been done, then we would never attach to wealth, name and fame. Attachment results in disputes, fights and strife, everywhere, only because people do not realise the Self. They do not realise that the Soul is the aim for which they have come to this Earth. Maybe some begin to think about it when it nibbles at them around the age of 50 years. In those who are ripe it will come even earlier as in the case of the Buddha, Shankaracharya, Ramana Maharishi and Swami Vivekananda. They come to show the path for a short time and then disappear. If they were to return now they would witness people all over the world lusting after material things.

This temptation has been called in this 36th verse **papam**, sin. This lust when it comes usually means that people are just dragged by force. It is difficult to renounce. What is the force which pushes individuals to do something which they would not like to do? This is the question asked in this verse.

In the first verse of this chapter (Chapter 3 of the **Srimad Bhagavad Gita**) Arjuna asked Sri Krishna: "If the path of knowledge is superior, then how is it that you are employing me in killing? Why do you not ask me to follow the path of **jnana yoga** which is so easy, and in which I do not have to involve myself in this great massacre?" Arjuna was horrified. We all have the same difficulties and it is to understand our condition that we study the **Bhagavad Gita**. The 35th verse was about **svadharma and paradharma.** You can only understand that these are relative terms, they speak about the Self and non-self. There is no line of demarcation between the Self and non-self, but, even then there is one, due to which conflict takes place in the minds of the people and leads to wars and riots. If people would realise that this is all God, then why would they fight? Gandhiji chanted every day the name of Iswara, God of Hindus, and Allah, God of Muslims, saying "Both names are Thy name". All religions in the beginning knew there was only one God but when difficult moments come in practical life then it is said, "he is a follower of

Allah" and "I am a follower of Iswara, Rama, Krishna", and there is a fight! This verse should be seen in a broad light, it does not only concern Arjuna. See it in the present circumstances of our life. We are all subjected to this conflict, this kind of lust. It may be lust for money, power or flesh.

So these terms **svadharma and paradharma, papam and punyam** – evil and good - are relative terms and exist only on the mental plane. In Self there is neither **papam** nor **punyam**. A person who is Self-realised is free to commit a sin but he will not commit it because sin does not exist in the Self. Bhagavan does not want to preach against **papam**, against evil, sin, but He wants to teach about the Self which is devoid of sin. The rest of the chapter will be devoted to answering Arjuna's second question just as Bhagavan Sri Krishna answered the first question up to the 35th verse.

By why is a man impelled to commit sin even when he does not want to, asks Arjuna. We do not want to become angry but we are; we do not want to become a victim of lust but we are. So there is conflict. Anger often comes like a sudden storm and you are not ready to receive it. Sometimes it does not have any reason – it comes and it goes. It seems to me that it is an energy stored in an individual. In Pure Self there is no anger but when there is an identification with anger you **become** angry. If you do not identify yourself with anger you do not become angry. Otherwise, if you see something happening as an objective reality and anger comes, you are a witness to it. Anger is not possible in pure "I" because anger is a passing mood and Self is not a passing mood – it is the Reality which exists in all the tenses, past, present and future.

Anger does not exist in all three tenses, that is why it is unreal, a passing phase, it is not eternal. Even before anger "I" existed, even when I become angry, "I" exists, and when anger passes away "I" exists, so it exists in all the three tenses. Anger is unreal, it is external and appears for a short time. You are bewildered; you begin to project yourself, just as in the darkness you see a rope and think it is a snake, you have a fearful response and try to run away. The snake does not exist in the rope. When you did not see the snake in the rope it did not exist, and when you saw the snake in the rope it also did not exist, it was simply not there. Anger comes in the same way. It is some kind of projection, like fear. Fear is also energy and is unreal because it appears and disappears. It is the same with anger also – it is the projection of the Pure Self. It does not exist in the Self, just as the snake does not exist in the rope. It is only an appearance, an illusion, and everybody is subjected to this kind of illusion in day-to-day life. When anger appears we lose Self-consciousness. The same happens when we see a snake in a rope.

Anger is a great problem for everybody. People are not abnormal, nor crazy, but at the time of being angry they appear to have lost all sense and do stupid things. A sincere **sadhaka** must scrutinize himself and find out where his anger is rooted. When the cause is known then at least it can be dealt with – that is why we do **sadhana**. So Arjuna's mind raises a question: "I do not want to commit sin, to become angry, because it plays havoc in my life, and for others. Then what is the reason, Krishna, for my becoming angry?" Changes take place from moment to moment, and we need to be a witness to changes. If we can be pure Witness then anger will not disturb us. We are Pure Self-awareness – we **are** the Self!

All that is required is acute, sharp Self-awareness and then you begin to live in harmony, you begin to flow. It is not something to be attained in the future, it is in the present. We must have clarity of thinking before real meditation arrives. A cloudy sky does not allow sunshine through. You should sit for meditation under the canopy of sky, by feeling the presence of the eternal sky, one enters in to the state of eternal consciousness. Don't sit always in a room, because from a room you may only see a small portion of the sky. Even, if there were windows all around the room you would still see only part of the sky. One thing more, clouds come and go but the blue sky remains. Meditation is something like the infinite blue sky when your mind becomes clear of all fogs, all thunderbolts. Divine meditation is inclusive, it excludes nothing. You can realise yourself according to your individual character, your composition, your inner and outer constitution, in a very simple way – just as you are doing.

Verse 37

श्री भगवानुवाच ।
काम एष क्रोध एष रजोगुणसमुद्भवः ।
महाशनो महापाप्मा विद्ध्येनमिह वैरिणम् ॥ ३७ ॥

Sri Bhagavan-uvāca I
kāma eṣa krodha eṣa rajoguṇa-samudbhavaḥ I
mahāśano mahāpāpmā viddhy-enam-iha vairiṇam II 37 II

Lord Krishna said, this is craving, this is wrath, born from the constituent Rajas. It is voracious, a great sin; know it to be the foe in this context.

kāmaḥ – desire; eṣaḥ – this; krodhaḥ – anger, wrath; eṣaḥ – this; rajoguna-samudbhavaḥ – born of the Rajo-guna; mahāśanaḥ – all-devouring, of great craving; mahāpāpmā – all sinfull; viddhi – know; enam – this; iha – here; vairiṇam – the foe, enemy.

Why is Bhagavan introducing the idea of desire in this 37th verse? He does so to point out the obstacles on the spiritual path. **Kamah** is desire, craving. What is craving? Craving, born of **rajoguna**, is to seize upon something which we feel we do not have. It is the limited life instinct for possession and satisfaction. Desires are motions of weakness and ignorance and they keep you chained to weakness and ignorance. It is very important that we understand, realise and experience the real meaning of craving so that we do not just criticize people. All individuals are pure in nature. In reality craving has nothing to do with the true nature with the Pure Self. Soul or Self cannot be impure, just as light cannot be impure – it is so subtle that no impurity can touch it. It is the same with the soul. Soul is pure love and devotion.

Arjuna asked Bhagavan Sri Krishna in the previous **sloka**: "By what is a man impelled, obliged, to commit sin (**papam**)?" In Sanskrit **papam** means something against which we must protect ourselves. By committing **papam** we involve ourselves in mental, emotional and physical problems of life. When desires are not fulfilled problems are created in society. If desire is not present, then evil is also not present. Desire is the cause, the source of all evil. Most people are motivated by desires. Permutations and combinations of these are the motivating forces of our activities and if not fulfilled we lose our temper and we are disturbed. Great troubles are created in everybody's lives – anger, jealousy, envy, hatred or violence comes. We begin to think that such and such a person is an enemy. Nobody is an enemy – do not condemn anyone! There is nothing to condemn in this world.

Maha aśanaḥ means great devourer whose appetite is enormous, and **maha-papma** means a great sin.

Bhagavan Sri Krishna says it is lust which is **mahasana**, which eats everything, everybody, like a demon. When a person becomes a victim of lust or anger he becomes demonic – you cannot imagine that he can be so different, so brutal.

Love is like light, and devotion like a moonlight night. Lust is like darkness, and yet where there is light darkness is also there. **Kama**, says Sri Krishna, is the great impediment to Divine Love. **Kama** means desire. Desire is the enemy of the whole world and, because of it, beings incur all evil. Desire when obstructed, interfered with in any way, turns into anger, hatred and jealousy. That's why **krodha** (anger) is also identical with this (desire). **Rajoguṇa-samudbhavaḥ**

– born of the **rajoguna**. When desire comes into being it instigates a person by arousing **rajas**. It is a state of consciousness which prevents us from realising the Self.

Try to eliminate lust or craving in any way possible. Devotional service and knowledge are the means to Self-realisation in order to cut off the **kama**.

Verse 38

धूमेनाव्रियते वह्निर्यथादर्शो मलेन च ।
यथोल्बेनावृतो गर्भस्तथा तेनेदमावृतम् ॥ ३८ ॥

Dhūmenā'vriyate vahnir-yathā'darśo malena ca I
yatho'lbenā'vṛto garbhas-tathā tene'dam āvṛtam II 38 II

As fire is covered by smoke, as a mirror by dust, as an embryo is enveloped by the womb, so is this (knowledge) covered by that (passion).

Dhūmena – by smoke; āvriyate – is enveloped, is covered; vahniḥ – fire; yathā – as; ādarśaḥ – a mirror; malena – by dust, dirt; ca – and; yathā – as; ulbena – in the womb by the amnion; āvṛtaḥ – enveloped; garbhaḥ – embryo, foetus; tathā – so; tena – by it; idam – this; āvṛtam – shrouded, covered.

In this verse Bhagavan Sri Krishna has taken three examples in order to explain craving, lust and passion. He explains how our lives are disturbed and how our Self-realisation is lost to sight when craving comes to us. The arrival of craving (of **Kama**) is the disappearance of the knowledge of the Self. An ordinary person is hypnotised by craving, a Self-aware person can never be attracted by craving. It is only when one forgets the Self that passion affects and influences us.

Dhūmenāvṛyate vahniḥ – As fire is covered by smoke, so is this knowledge covered by desire. Where there is smoke there is fire also. When we see smoke we think or imagine that there is a fire even though we do not see the fire. So fire and smoke are born together – in the same wood there is fire and smoke! Smoke has a dark complexion, black or grey in colour, and it affects our eyes. They fill with tears and we cannot see through the smoke, it obstructs our vision. In contrast, fire is light. It does not obstruct our vision, nor brings tears to our eyes and we can see in the presence of fire.

In the same way when there is a desire (desire has been compared with smoke), or passion for something, it is the desire which obstructs our vision and prevents an evaluation of an object. When desire is born, even the intellect of the nature of goodness is covered by desire as fire by smoke, so then the intellect of the mode of passion and ignorance will definitely be covered by it. As soon as a desire is born, the spiritual path is covered with its smoke. If it is given scope for enhancement, it makes the path totally dark. The desire veils discrimination. Just as fire can burn even when it is covered with smoke, so can discrimination work if a man becomes cautious as soon as desire is born.

So you can see that though smoke and fire have the same root, the properties of one are dark and **tamasic** in nature, and the other is light-coloured and **sattvic** in nature. Light dispels darkness. The knowledge of Self has been compared to the flame, and the smoke to desire. Both exist in the same human being, but one of them is enlightenment and the other is darkness.

So, those people who are wise take care. In order to make wise decisions the mind must be devoid of darkness. When it is infatuated it is very difficult to make the right decision. That is why decisions made in a moment of passion can bring suffering and depression. We all experience this in daily life and yet, surprisingly, over and over again the same mistakes are committed. We suffer because we run after the pleasures of life and when pain comes, as it is bound to come, we suffer. After pleasure pain follows. So, it is **Kama** (passion) that forces a person to run after all these objects outside and makes him unstable and restless. **Kama** is born out of **rajoguna**, one of the qualities of **prakriti**.

If you are in the position to conquer, to subdue, to replace this **rajoguna** then do so. It will not be removed by darkness and ignorance, by sleeping over, by not thinking, by not facing the situation. When we sit here in **satsanga** we are in **sattvaguna** – the nature of which is illumination and light – and we are trying to subdue this **rajoguna** through knowledge and there is a possibility of sublimation. It is for this purpose that we sit here, that this Self-consciousness may appear in us. We begin to realise that if this **rajoguna** is not subdued, it will take us away from the right path as the wind takes a sailing boat in all directions, even in the direction opposite to your destination. In the same way, passions and desires take us away from our goal of life. It is a daily experience and people suffer afterwards because every action has a consequence. Our future life is a consequence of our past life, of past reactions.

While performing actions in thoughts, words and deeds we have to be careful. As to what kind of a present and future we want to have, it depends upon us to a very great extent. It's not that we do not have freedom of will – we do. For example, if we want to swim to the other shore we may be swept away by a strong current. But some swimmers do not go straight – they swim across the current but also swim with the current, and the point at which the swimmer arrives on the other shore will be the result of his own effort and the action of the current upon him. So also in our own lives. If freedom of will is not there, or if it is determined to some extent by our past actions and behaviour, we can now accumulate the energy in order to cross the river of life to our own destination, however difficult it may be.

It is for that purpose that we stay here in the ashram, where we may rest and relax and accumulate energy so that we may go exactly where we want to go, and not be swept away by the current of passions, desires and ambitions. It is not an easy task to see through the illusions that desires bring. For that we need the guidance and help of a master and the help of these beautiful treatises on Yoga and meditation, such as the **Bhagavad Gita**. Instructions from a teacher, even from the **Bhagavad Gita**, to "realise the Self" can be misinterpreted very easily and the listener may understand that they can do whatever they like. Those people who want to realise the Self by only reading the translations and commentaries can be led in wrong directions. By studying it slowly with a master, slowly the teaching becomes clearer. Alert attention is required so that we may seize what the teachings say and mean to say. The deeper significance of the teachings of Lord Krishna's words is present but only an acute intelligence can seize it.

The path of Self-realisation is such a slippery path that anyone can easily forget Self-awareness. Great saints did not forget – in all that they did they were always Self-aware. The external behaviour, the conduct, did not obstruct their continuous process of Self-awareness. In **Samadhi** (meditation), when Self-awareness comes, it is never lost again when once attained, but attaining it is a very difficult task.

So, be careful; as the fire is in the wood, so it is in you also. Self is not outside you, just as fire is not outside the wood. Just as the fire is not outside the wood, smoke also isn't. So where there is Self and Self-enlightenment there is also desire and passion which does not allow us to realise clearly the nature of the Pure Self.

Yathādarśo malena ca is another example given in this verse. When dirt accumulates on the surface of a mirror, it can't reflect an object. Similarly, the dirt of desire veils knowledge and a striver can't decide what he ought to do and what he ought not to do.

Sages have tried to explain what Self-realisation is. You can see a reflection of your body but the soul is so subtle it cannot be reflected in a mirror – you can't see the soul with your eyes. Your mind is like a mirror and dust is like a passion, a desire. So, Lord Krishna is trying to make you understand what is passion and what the Self is, and how it is that passion obstructs your Self-realisation.

So, as dust covers the surface of a mirror, the Self will not be seen unless the mind is cleaned. That is why we do **Sadhana** – to defeat the foes like lust, hatred, anger, greed, infatuation and jealousy, on the path of Self-realization. Many try to move on the divine path, but out of many thousands there is hardly one who finishes the race. Some go fast, get tired and sleep, others move slowly, patiently and with perseverance, and reach the goal.

So you can understand in this second example that our mind is like a mirror and the dust is like strong desire and passion that covers – veils – the surface of our mind and does not allow us to see clearly through to the Self.

Yatholbenavṛto garbhaḥ – The embryo is covered with the amnion so much that it can't even see or move inside the amnion, and is cut off from contact with the outside world. He has the means of realisation – the sense perception or the knowledge of the external world – but they are all closed. At least in the first two examples the individual had more freedom to use the five sense perceptions to obtain knowledge of this world, which later on helps towards Self-realisation; whereas the embryo is covered with the amnion like an envelope, and contained within the womb. This example points to an individual who is lost completely in inertia, where there is no open expectation for self-awareness. Self-awareness in an embryo is difficult to detect, and Self-realisation still more. Inertia does not allow us to realise the Self. We are absorbed in inertia, that's why the right kind of meditation does not come to us. It will only come when we have transcended inertia which is like an embryo. Although we have come out of our mother's womb we are in the cosmic womb of the Divine Mother. As long as Self-realisation has not dawned upon us, we are still in the amnion of the Divine Mother, the Divine Nature.

Verse 39

आवृतं ज्ञानमेतेन ज्ञानिनो नित्यवैरिणा ।
कामरूपेण कौन्तेय दुष्पूरेणानलेन च ॥ ३९ ॥

Āvṛtaṁ jnānam-etena jñānino nityavairiṇā I
kāmarūpeṇa kaunteya duṣpūreṇānalena ca II 39 II

Knowledge, O son of Kunti (Arjuna), is obscured by this persistent foe of the knower, i.e. by craving, as by an insatiable fire.

āvṛtaṁ – enveloped, covered; jñānaṁ – knowledge; etena – by this; jñāninaḥ – of the wise, of the knower; nityavairiṇā – by the constant enemy; kāmarūpeṇa – whose form is desire; kaunteya – O Kaunteya, O son of Kunti; duṣpūreṇa – unappeasable, insatiable; analena – by fire; ca – and.

Knowledge is covered or enveloped by desire. Desire growing to greed is a destructive force and an enemy to all human beings. To the ignorant, of course, at the time of enjoyment, desire is the cause of pleasure. But to the wise, the knower of the Self, who remembers harm in it, it is the cause of pain alone, even at that time. Therefore it is said to be their eternal enemy. Being a fire, it is so hard to satisfy, very hard to quench. If one is unaware of Self it is due to craving, **kama**. In the previous verse Bhagavan Sri Krishna gave three similes, smoke, dust and amnion. All three represent craving. When dust is removed from the mirror you can see your own reflection, but the condition is that the mirror and you should be in light. The mirror may be free of dust but if you are standing in darkness, then also you cannot see! Heart and mind must be purified in order to have knowledge and awareness. The mind must be quiet. If it is not, then knowledge of the Self does not come. It takes time to bring the mind to quietude, to realise the beauty of the Self. Most of the time we are extroverted – how can we realise the Self when we are pulled by desires?

When we sit here for some time in meditation and studying beautiful scriptures we are not running after satisfaction of our desires somewhere else. Satisfaction of a desire brings happiness for a few moments only. There is a strong urge in human beings for eternal peace and happiness, the very nature of the Self. But instead of seeking it in the Self, we are seeking it somewhere else.

When desires are not fulfilled we become angry, filled with hatred and jealousy, and we do and say hurtful things. Afterwards we repent and ask ourselves, "Why did we do that?" When Self-awareness comes the person reflects upon the incident as to how and why it occurred.

For one who lives in Self-awareness there is no anger, hatred or jealousy. They do not exist in the Self. It is only when the ego identifies with anger that we become angry. If the ego were to identify with the Self we would not become angry. We are Self-aware only in the present – it does not come in the future.

So we sit here in the present, and Bhagavan's words of wisdom are an impetus to us, a source of knowledge and wisdom which dawns upon us. The examples, similes, given by Bhagavan are full of deep significance. Even through smoke you can see part of the flame. So, in the state of meditation, of reflecting and thinking, you are partly aware of the Self, even if craving is there. But in the example of the embryo covered with amnion, it cannot make any effort inside the envelope of membrane (amnion), it is completely imprisoned. It has to wait till it is free.

Such is not the case with the flame and the mirror – at least there is a possibility of seeing – but when an embryo is covered with amnion it is completely obscured.

A person who is completely absorbed in the material life is incapable of seeing the Self. He is under the governance of **prakriti**. The material life covers his reason just as the amnion covers the embryo. So many people are in that condition and it is not possible for them to meditate – so many fears disturb them. They can do **asanas** to quieten the body and the mind and in that way prepare further for meditation. So it is good for us to spend time in an ashram, to take time for practising **asanas**, meditation and participating in **satsanga**. The benefits you will realise later, if not now.

Satsanga does not mean just the reading of the **Bhagavad Gita**. Many people read it like parrots, or just mumble like priests. In **satsanga** you become aware of the real Self which is your real nature. Reading, repetition, chanting, of the **Bhagavad Gita** is not having **Satsanga**. **Satsanga** is having attachment with the Truth, and Truth is Pure Self – **Atman.**

Verse 40

इन्द्रियाणि मनो बुद्धिरस्याधिष्ठानमुच्यते ।
एतैर्विमोहयत्येष ज्ञानमावृत्य देहिनम् ॥ ४० ॥

Indriyāṇi mano buddhir-asyādhiṣṭhānam-ucyate I
etair-vimohayaty-eṣa jñānam-āvṛtya dehinam II 40 II

Its abode is said to be the senses, mind and intellect. By means of these it obscures knowledge and deludes the embodied man.

indriyāṇi – the senses, the organs; manaḥ – the mind; buddhiḥ – the intellect; asya – its; adhiṣṭhānam – seat, abode; ucyate – is called; etaiḥ – by these; vimohayati – deludes, bewilders; eṣaḥ – this; jñānam – knowledge; āvṛtya – having enveloped, covering, by veiling; dehinam – the embodied being.

The organs, the five senses, the mind and the intellect are the three dwelling places of desire, and can delude the embodied soul. So the dwelling places of desires are also the dwelling places of delusion. The activities of the five organs, the mind and the intellect are the medium for the expression of desire. Desire covers the knowledge of the Self by stimulating these. When you are doing **sadhana** – think of it and find out where the desire dwells. Desire arises through seeing, hearing, smelling, touching and tasting sense objects; through thinking of sense objects and through a determination regarding them. When we experience the world the students of experiences are the senses, which also become the subject matter of illusion. So the individual soul is deluded.

What is the difference between mind and intellect? In intellect there is discrimination and in mind there is not. In ordinary cases the **buddhi** (intellect) lies dormant, it is sleeping. Inquiry, seeking, awakens it, otherwise its tendency is to be inert. Mind has the capability of thinking but has no discrimination between right and wrong. After experience, the mind becomes **buddhi** because it is through experience that we come to know what is right and what is wrong. That is the task of **buddhi.**

The senses even torment **Hatha Yoga** practitioners. That's why, first of all, the senses should be conquered and controlled. When the senses are controlled the mind will, by itself, stop running about and the discerning intellect will be set free and lust and anger lose their support. Otherwise, when the senses are excited by their objects they create restlessness or violent disturbance. They carry away the mind-sense just as the wind carries away a ship on the sea. In the same way, the mind subjected to the emotions, passions and longings, carries away the intelligence which loses its power of calm discrimination and mastery.

Such is the function of desire (**kama**). Bhagavan Sri Krishna has spoken of its rising and disappearance, and how it deludes the individual soul. These are beautiful **slokas** and very important for our **sadhana**. Bhagavan Sri Krishna is building the path of Self-realisation for you so that you can walk on it with understanding.

When you are sitting in meditation you are trying to withdraw the senses. Now, how do we begin to deal with them? Firstly, we discipline ourselves. We discipline the mind. A mind which is confused and disturbed can never meditate. Lord Patanjali says in one of his **sutras: tajjapastadartha-bhāvanam** (Yoga Sutras 1.28) – when the mantra "**Aum**" is repeated constantly with deep feeling and full understanding of the meaning, it helps the **sadhaka** to reach the highest state in Yoga. When we do **Japa** and repetition of a mantra, the mind gets filled with **sattwa** (purity, light). It helps one to discover the Self and slowly remove the impediments to Self-realisation. The mind gets purified and knowledge of the real essential nature is discovered. We realise that the Self in us is different from the body, senses, mind, intellect and ego.

The "Aum" mantra is considered to be **sabda Brahman**, the word of God or the universal sound. Patanjali says: **tasya vācakaḥ praṇavaḥ** – God, the Absolute, is represented by the sacred syllable **aum** (**pranava**). "OM" is enjoined in the **Vedas** and the **Upanishads** as the most suitable sound symbol for the Divine, the Self. It is the root of all mantras. Sound is the vibration which is at the source of all creation. But God, the Absolute, is beyond vibration but vibration is the subtlest form of His creation, the only way to go near Him, to reach Him. That is why we take His symbol.

So if we want to transcend this mundane consciousness, then the way is to discipline our senses, mind and intellect which is the art of **sadhana**.

Verse 41

तस्मात्त्वमिन्द्रियाण्यादौ नियम्य भरतर्षभ।
पाप्मानं प्रजहि ह्येनं ज्ञानविज्ञाननाशनम्॥ ४१॥

Tasmāt-tvam-indriyāṇy-ādau niyamya bharatarṣabha I
pāpmānaṁ prajahi hy-enaṁ jñānavijñāna-nāśanam II 41 II

Therefore, O Best of Bharatas (Arjuna), control thy senses and slay this sinful destroyer of wisdom and discrimination.

tasmāt – therefore; tvam – you; indriyāṇi – the senses; the organs; ādau – in the beginning; niyamya – having controlled, by regulating; bharatarṣabha – O best of the Bharata-race; pāpmānam – the sinful; prajahi – kill, curb; hi – surely; enam – this; jñānavijñāna-nāśanam – the destroyer of the knowledge and realisation.

Bhagavan tells Arjuna to control and discipline the senses in the beginning and then slay lust. A small child is completely devoid of lust and desire. He is an **Ajātaśatru – ajata** means non-born, **satru** means foe, which means there is nobody in the world who is born as a foe for him. People become older, but they are still incapable of disciplining their senses and minds, and so desire, lust, or craving remain. When desires are curbed, when there is no more craving and lust is no longer rampant, the human being becomes completely spotless. All becomes uncontaminated, completely pure, spotlessly clean. Spots are due to scum – craving, desire, lust. When these are not present there is no sin and consequently, no sinner.

Bhagavan Sri Krishna is showing a way out, a path away from the clutches of desire. This path is for everyone. In the previous **sloka** the abode of desire – senses, mind and intellect – was mentioned. To uproot desire Bhagavan tells us to discipline the senses. A person who is undisciplined sees something and runs after it like a small child. They follow their senses – their senses do not follow them! A self-disciplined person governs the senses. A worldly man runs after sense objects irrespective of the consequences; he lacks awareness. As you sow so you reap – the law of action governs all of us. So we must be very careful before we act because by what we think, say and do, we create our own future. We can make or mar it – it depends upon us.

Our senses are like horses, and our body like a chariot. If we do not hold the reins properly, or drive the horses properly, they can lead us to heinous consequences. It is a very great responsibility to drive this chariot, this body. Bhagavan Sri Krishna is the driver of Arjuna's chariot and Arjuna is sitting inside it. The chariot is the symbol of the individual soul. In this body is an individual soul on a pilgrimage, a divine journey. With Bhagavan as the driver of Arjuna's chariot there is no fear, no risk, no danger. Victory is ours when we surrender the reins into divine hands, we surrender to our real Self – we simply do not know that! We are dominated by ego, we are blind and arrogant. Ego drives our chariot which is why there are risks, there are pitfalls and ditches into which the horses tumble. If Bhagavan Sri Krishna drives the chariot, then where is the problem? Hand the reins to Bhagavan and then your senses are under control and disciplined.

The real Self is the abode of knowledge; the senses, mind and intellect are the abode of desire. We do not know this so we are groping in darkness, living in mire and full of suffering. In the absence of this knowledge happiness is lost. Self-realisation is your birthright but you forget it in a fast changing world. An undisciplined mind can create havoc. What disciplines the mind? The movements of a mighty elephant are directed by a small pointed weapon used by its driver, the mahout. So can this powerful mind be governed under the occupation of **Japa**, of meditation.

The great saints lived in peace, their senses silenced, conquered by these holy men and women. The senses did not make saints dance. An ordinary person dances in the hands of the senses, as does this whole world in the cosmic dance. We can be just like a puppet in the hands of the senses when they are not controlled. The world outside is an expression of your **citta vritti** (movements in the consciousness) but you think it is independent of you completely! We run after worldly objects like small ignorant children! Some of these objects, of course, are necessities of life, but many are not. The wise person will differentiate. Remember that we are the creators of this fast-paced world with all its inventions and regulations! We cannot condemn it. If you don't like it you can leave it for a short time. Cross the river here, go into the hills and experience how life is there. See the shepherds and observe how quietly they live in the world, looking after their animals. They used to give us goat milk to drink for free, but nowadays those who live close to the town are more interested in selling the milk. So it is changing, but we can still find calm places where we can be isolated. But not for a long time, because we also need to participate in the life of cities.

Woods and forests have been the cradles of civilization in India. All our great scriptures have their roots in the forests, in these golden cradles where knowledge has evolved in a peaceful atmosphere. When mind is at peace it evolves in a right, rich and prosperous way. A great culture evolved in India which has universal application. Who does not know the **Vedas?** The other day we were studying Sanskrit literature and I was surprised to find how many people outside India have contributed to its growth by writing, translating, and editing the classical texts.

Here we study the **Bhagavad Gita** which is the key to all the sacred scriptures in India. It is deep and profound and requires much reflection. In a condensed form it is like clarified butter, ghee. From a lot of milk you create a small amount of butter and ghee. In the same way this **Bhagavad Gita** is like butter and ghee. It is a supreme nectar which gives you immortality! But people run after other tastes, governed by their senses. They are proud of their bad habits sometimes, habits which are often inconsiderate of other people. Smoking, for example, is one such habit – people are addicted to it and seem not to care that they are responsible for an unpleasant odour which offends others, and clings to the clothes and skin of the smoker and non-smokers. And what an expensive habit it is in terms of money and time, such costly time because it will never come back to us. Our master says that time is invaluable, it is running out. You cannot catch hold of it. Time wasted on valueless things will be repented when a person grows old and is physically infirm. This is only commonsense.

And it is commonsense which Bhagavan is speaking. He is giving nectar to Arjuna and to all of us because He loves us, loves all humankind. In this world people are so restless, discontented and dissatisfied, only because of desires. Desires are the cause of all sufferings and cessation of desire is the cessation of all sufferings. This philosophy is the core teaching of Lord Buddha and of what you are drinking today – **Gitamritam**, nectar of the **Gita** – given to us by Bhagavan Sri Krishna.

jahi śatruṁ kāmarūpam – Slay this great destroyer of wisdom and knowledge, of Self-realisation!

Verse 42

इन्द्रियाणि पराण्याहुरिन्द्रियेभ्यः परं मनः ।
मनसस्तु परा बुद्धिर्यो बुद्धेः परतस्तु सः ॥ ४२ ॥

Indriyāṇi parāṇyāhur-indriyebhyaḥ paraṁ manaḥ I
manasas-tu parā buddhir-yo buddheḥ paratas-tu saḥ II 42 II

> *They say that the senses are noble; nobler than the senses is the mind. Intellect is even nobler than the mind. What is nobler, still, than the intellect is the He, the Self.*

Indriyāni – the senses, the five organs: ear, etc.; parāṇi – superior; āhuḥ – they say; indriyebhyaḥ – than the senses; param – superior; manaḥ – the mind; manasaḥ – than the mind; tu – but; parā – superior; buddhiḥ – intellect; yaḥ – who; buddheḥ – than the intellect; parataḥ – greater; tu – but; saḥ – He.

Indriyāṇi parāṇyāhuḥ – Senses are superior to the body or objects of senses. The senses know the objects but the objects don't know the senses. For example, the eyes can perceive the physical body and objects, but the body and objects can't perceive the senses. The senses are greater, more powerful and more subtle than the objects and the physical body.

Indriyebhyaḥ paraṁ manaḥ – Senses don't know the mind, while the mind knows all the senses. Every sense knows only its own object. Ears for example can perceive only sound but not touch, form, taste, etc. The mind knows the five senses and their objects. That's why the mind is superior, more powerful, more subtle than the senses.

Manasastu parā buddhiḥ – The mind does not know the intellect but the intellect knows the mind and senses. The intellect knows if the mind is quiet or not, if the senses function properly or not. It knows the mind and the thoughts, as well as the senses and their objects. Therefore, the intellect is greater, more powerful, more subtle than the mind.

Yo buddheḥ paratastu saḥ – The master of intellect is the ego. Intellect is an instrument and ego is the doer. Desire resides in ego. Ego has the desire to enjoy pleasures and becomes the enjoyer. There is no desire in the Self. Body, mind, senses, intellect and ego are fragments of nature (**prakriti**). The Self is the base, the root, the cause, the inspirer of the body, senses, mind, intellect and ego and is subtler, greater, stronger than all of them.

The final reality is of transcendental character. Self transcends body, mind and intellect. Desire dwells in senses, mind and intellect. If there is anything which transcends the intellect, it is the Pure Self, **Atman.** That is why we cannot conquer desires with the help of the senses, body, mind and intellect, because they do not transcend desire. If there is anything which transcends them all it's the Self alone.

That is why the person who has transcended up to the intellect has been able to transcend desire with the help of the Self alone. Self is a transcendental reality. So if we want to transcend desire the only possibility left to us is Self-realisation. Only a Self-realised person is able to transcend desire, lust, craving. A person who lives on the mental (intellectual), sensuous or physical plane is not capable of transcending desire, because they are all the planes where desire dwells. Self is not the dwelling place of desire. In Self the desire doesn't dwell. It's not the abode of desire. Take care and think of it, it is very important in the process of our **Sadhana**. By and by we transcend desire with the help of the senses, body with the help of the mind, and with the help of intellect the mind, and with the help of the Self we transcend the intellect, and having lived up to the level of intellect, desire is also transcended. How to transcend the body? There must be something more transcendental than the body. With the help of the mind you are able to transcend the body and senses. Most people live on the physical plane. They work through the senses and they stay there. They don't go further, they are not capable of transcending the sensuous plane. They live on the sensuous plane of consciousness and they are confined to it. A few persons are left who go further to reach the mental plane. All our studying is done on the mental plane. It is the great scholars who remain there. All creations of art, philosophy, knowledge are confined to the mental and intellectual plane. That's why those who transcend the senses come to the mental plane and when they go further, they come to the intellectual plane.

Niscayātmika-buddhiḥ means the intellect which takes only one decision and that decision is Self-realisation, with the help of sense discrimination. People climb up to the intellectual plane, but they do not go further. It remains their zenith. Wise men, even great scholars, remain on this plane. They don't transcend it. The transcendental plane is not in their periphery, it's not in their circumference. They just live on the circumference of the intellectual plane, they don't transcend it, while a real Yogi, a Self-enlightened person, even transcends the intellect. It is only on the spiritual plane, on the path of Self-realisation that a person is capable of eliminating desire.

When you meditate, think of this procedure and step by step try to arrive in the infinite, vast, subtle-like sky, a still further level of consciousness, which can be called the Self. Although it is beyond words, the **Upanishads** say: "Self is that from which the speech recoils. It is unattainable by the mind." Self is not attained only by the help of the mind. The Self cannot be realised through studying, reading and writing. You may think you have realised the Self but the Self still plays hide and seek with you. It doesn't come within the reach of the mental and intellect. That's why even great scholars or wise men have to meditate. In meditation the mind and intellect are transcended. That's why it is called transcendental or divine meditation, or Brahma Samadhi in which the Divine is realised.

When we sit in meditation, thoughts do come. Let them come. By and by even thoughts are eliminated. They are just like sparks coming out of the Self, but they are not Self. Self is still different.

In the mind, up to the mental sheath, all kinds of imaginations come. The whole past impressions and ideas unfold themselves. The mental sheath unfolds itself. Allow it to unfold – it takes some time. Let the impressions of the past come. When it has become purified, all imaginations of the past (good and bad) are washed off. Sometimes people stop their meditation or they give up, but they should not. These are the obstacles and at the same time the stepping stones. To a weak person they are obstacles, but a strong person transcends them and goes beyond. They don't stay there. They who transcend the mental plane are energetic and mighty minded. They reach the intellectual level of consciousness in which there is oneness, which is called **niscayātmikā buddhiḥ**, where the decision takes place: "I have to realise the Self now."

What is this **buddhih** which is different from the mind? This mind is the mental sheath in which the individual has come out. More subtle and nobler is the intellect's sheath that covers consciousness, that covers the individual.

Kama (desire) dwells in all these bodies, senses, mind and intellect. So they are all occupied by desire, craving and lust. If even the intellect fails, what is there to say of the sensuous plane and the mental one?

So, up to the intellectual plane, lust, craving, desire are not defeated, they remain. The foe is not outside. All our foes are self-created and come from **kama**. A person who is desireless is **aparājitaḥ**. He is an **ajātaśatru**, which means he is a person who has no anger, because he has no desire – he is in a desireless state of consciousness and will never have a mean thought. Such a person has transcended enemity. Even enemies will be transformed into friends.

Verse 43

We conclude chapter three by going back to the beginning of it with Arjuna's questioning to Bhagavan Sri Krishna as to why He wants Arjuna to fight.

Starting with **Karma Yoga** Bhagavan asks Arjuna to perform devotional services because it is the easiest art for Self-realisation for worldly people. Arjuna is the representative, symbol, of individuals who are living normally in this world. Bhagavan suggests to Arjuna to follow the path of devotional services. In devotional services through actions the devotee becomes one with the Divine as He lives in all, in every human being. The way of worship becomes to render our services in our humble capacity, and our devotional services, thinking that He lives in each one of us, become a means to Self-realization. He lives in each one of us, but only a devotee can realise it through his devotional activities, through his dedicated and loving activities – because actions performed in love and devotion are transformed as the means of communication and as the means of union with the Divine. This union with the Divine through devotional activities is called Yoga. You can call it **Karma, Bhakti** or **Jnana Yoga**.

Arjuna is gifted as a ***Karmayogi*** and it is also his station in life. The relation between Arjuna, the individual soul, and Bhagavan Sri Krishna, the Divine, is a very close relation. When we live together we come closer and we know each other more and more. In the beginning it is difficult to know, everything looks all right, but when we come closer difficulties sometimes arise. This was also the case between Krishna and Arjuna. Krishna is Bhagavan and He has boundless love for His devotees, infinite love, patience and perseverance. He knows how to wait, how to have patience and perseverance. Perseverance is a great thing. It doesn't come so easily – we become impatient if the work is not done quickly and we lose temper. The spiritual, the divine evolution in every individual is not so fast; material evolution outside is very fast, but the evolution that takes place inside the individual either on the intellectual or the emotional or spiritual plane is different and that is why there is a psychic tension existing in us, in society, all over the world. To establish that equilibrium, that balance in the inner world and the outer world, is a difficult task.

Bhagavan Sri Krishna is omniscient. He knows all, He knows the heart and mind of His disciples, His devotees, His friends. He loves them all. Love is not an ordinary force. It is the motivating force of the whole universe – that's why love is God and God is love. The relation of Bhagavan, the master, is not only the relation of the teacher and the taught, He is also a great lover. Love can not be learned. It is so natural and spontaneous and is given to everybody. Bhagavan shows us what real love is and how real love can be possible between the teacher and the taught, the master and disciple. The position of Bhagavan Sri Krishna is of a master, and the position of Arjuna is of the disciple. He is showing the way. He is removing the hurdles – the obstacles which are coming in his individual, private and personal life – and at the same time not showing that He is superior to Arjuna. That's why He establishes a friendly relation also, because friends are equal. Friendship is only possible when equal combinations are there. If one is superior and one is inferior in any field, friendship is difficult.

एवं बुद्धेः परं बुद्ध्वा संस्तभ्यात्मानमात्मना ।
जहि शत्रुं महाबाहो कामरूपं दुरासदम् ॥ ४३ ॥

Evaṁ buddheḥ paraṁ buddhvā
samstabhyā'tmānam ātmanā I
jahi śatruṁ mahābāho
kāmarūpaṁ durāsadam II 43 II

O mighty-armed Arjuna! Thus realising that, which is beyond the reason, and controlling the Self (mind) by the Self (intellect), destroy this enemy, which is difficult to conquer, in the shape of desire.

Evam – thus, as; buddheḥ – than the intellect; param – superior; buddhvā – having known, understanding; saṁstabhya – restraining, completely establishing; ātmānam – the Self; ātmanā – by the Self; jahi – slay thou, vanquish; śatrum – the enemy; mahābāho – O mighty-armed; kāmarūpam – of the form of desire; durāsadam – hard to conquer, difficult to subdue.

The mind can control all the organs and the physical body. The gross cannot control the finer and so the mind cannot control the intellect, whereas the **buddhi**, intellect, can control the mind. When the mind is held firm and steady, so that it dissociates from the sense organs, then the passion is automatically overcome as the passion has no reality except when the mind is observing and feeding on it.

In order to perform all actions according to our own religion, for universal welfare, without attachment in the form of desire, we must have perfect control over the senses. Lord Krishna does not say one should forcibly kill the senses and give up all actions. No, the purpose of the senses is to collect the impressions of the external world and after the mind has coordinated them, the reason distinguishes between them and the Atman, the Self is beyond all these and different from all these.

Evam buddheḥ paraṁ buddhvā – Know that *param*, that Supreme, the Divine Reality. The final solution of the problem is by realisation of the Supreme, that Divine Reality. Accept any path, according to your temperament, to the constitution of your nature. Let it be the path of devotional service, **karmayoga**, the path of knowledge, **jnanayoga,** or of devotion, **bhaktiyoga**, or any other. There are so many, as many as individuals. Paths are immaterial, it's the destination which counts. All the paths lead to the same destination – the common goal. So having known what transcends the intellect and mind, intellect is purified and it is in that purified intellect that the sun of wisdom dawns upon us. How to purify the mind and intellect has been mentioned in the previous **slokas**. When the mind merges into the intellect and when the intellect is purified, then it is devoid of arrogance, hatred, malaise, jealousy, envy. It is crystal clear, it becomes pure and takes the reflection of the Divine. The transparent and clean, purified intellect becomes like a drop of dew and whatever blade of grass it may be on, it doesn't matter, but the whole sun, the Divine, is reflected in it. And it is only in the divine state of consciousness that desire and craving do not exist any more.

People have tried to conquer anger, hatred, jealousy, envy through various means but they have failed. The history of spiritual life has been a failure. Why? Because they do not know the simple reality that there is a divine principle which exists in this entire universe, in this cosmos. It is this cosmic consciousness which exists in the form of divine love, knowledge and divine action.

Our task is to purify our minds and intellect. This is our work, nobody will do it for us. When our hearts, minds and intellect are purified, then this reflection takes place and the darkness is dispelled. Then we can contemplate on what is beyond all this. Awareness comes in the Pure Self. When there is Pure Self-awareness then there is Self-enlightenment, knowledge of the Self is attained and the soul abides safe in the bliss of the Self.

Thus ends the third chapter of the **Bhagavad Gita** entitled **Karma Yoga** or the Art of Working.